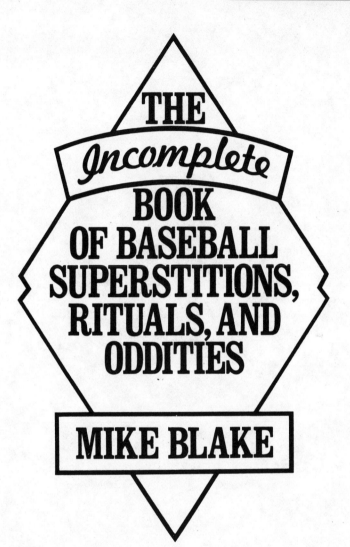

THE *Incomplete* BOOK OF BASEBALL SUPERSTITIONS, RITUALS, AND ODDITIES

MIKE BLAKE

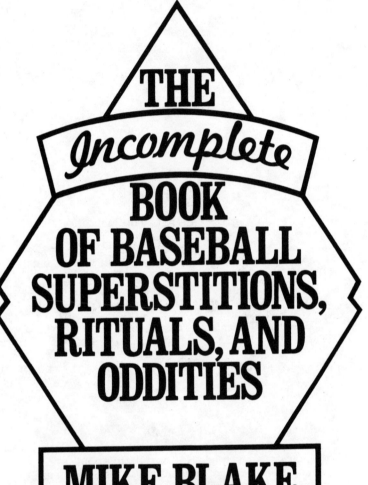

THE *Incomplete* BOOK OF BASEBALL SUPERSTITIONS, RITUALS, AND ODDITIES

MIKE BLAKE

WYNWOOD® Press
New York, New York

Library of Congress Cataloging-in-Publication Data

Blake, Mike.
    The incomplete book of baseball superstitions, rituals, and
oddities / Mike Blake.
       p.   cm.
    Includes bibliographical references (p.   ) and index.
    ISBN 0-922066-59-0
    1. Baseball—Anecdotes. 2. Baseball players—Anecdotes.
I. Title.
GV873.B57 1991
796.357′0207—dc20

                                            90-46681
                                              CIP

Copyright © 1991 by Mike Blake
Published by WYNWOOD Press
An imprint of Gleneida Publishing Group, Inc.
New York, New York
Printed in the United States of America

To my wife, Jan, who puts up with my own oddities, rituals, and idiosyncrasies while exhibiting enough of her own to keep me laughing; my daughter, Kim, and son, Greg, who compete with their dad for funny behavior; Mom and Dad, who made me as odd as I am today; Cliff and Merle, who don't take backseats to anyone in terms of entertaining habits; and all those great diamond heroes of the past and present, who prove that truth is stranger than fiction.

Contents

Acknowledgments

Wynwood Press (New York), my kind, benevolent, and not-so-odd publisher, has allowed me to thank everyone who made this book possible: the storytellers, the storymakers, the storylivers, and those associated with the grand old game of baseball who make it the funniest and most enduring sport on the third planet from the sun.

The author, superstitious enough to heed all attorneys' advice, hereby wishes to gratefully acknowledge all of those information providers and contact sharers whose help, real or imagined, was preyed upon during the research phase of this book.

This offbeat but generous squad of baseball lovers includes Richard Re (Wynwood Press), who went out on a limb to accept this book; Jon Miller (Baltimore Orioles and ESPN), a kind and very funny broadcaster who introduced me to other funny broadcasters; Joe Torre (California Angels and St. Louis Cardinals), a witty, helpful baseball analyst with a keen baseball mind and a warm heart for journalists trying to do their jobs; Ernie Harwell (Detroit Tigers), an unselfish and marvelous recaller of jocular times; Vin Scully (Los Angeles Dodgers), what a voice, and what a storyteller; Phil Rizzuto (New York Yankees), "Holy Cow," can this guy tell 'em; Al Conin (California Angels), who's been humorous since we went to elementary school together; Mike Terry (*San Bernardino Sun*), who whimsically "got into" the subject matter of this book; Buzzie Bavasi (California Angels), who has helped me out in the past and aided me again on this project with his knowledge, contacts, and kindness; Julian John Portman, my agent and business partner, who spins great yarns and has a wonderful sense of what is comical; the late Harley "Ace" Tinkham (*Los Angeles Times*), who had a wonderful memory and a knack for humor; Bob Costas (NBC); Pam Reichman; and all those writers, newscasters, players, and hangers-on who shared one-liners with me before those many ballgames at Anaheim Stadium and Dodger Stadium.

Also of great, odd, superstitious, and ritualistic help to me were Kevin Rhomberg (Cleveland Indians); Dave Parker (Milwaukee Brewers); Joe Black (former Brooklyn Dodger, MLB, Greyhound Corp.); Richard Levin (Major League Baseball—The Commissioner's Office); Phyllis Merhige (American League); Katy Feeney (National League); Bob Broeg (Society for American Baseball Research, or SABR, *St. Louis Post-Dispatch,* KMOX radio); Roy Firestone (ESPN); Jim Skipper (SABR); Gene Mauch (California Angels); Normal "Tweed" Webb (Negro Leagues); Phil Dixon (SABR); Ron Fairly (San Francisco Giants); Dave Cunningham (*Long Beach Press Telegram*); Bob Hoie (SABR); Stu Nahan (KTLA-TV and KABC radio) (I beat him twice as an opposing goalie on the ice in Van Nuys, but Stu is still the best cigar-smoking goalie I ever saw); Bill Valentine (Arkansas Travelers); Red Patterson, Jimmie Reese, Bert Blyleven, Doug Rader, Moose Stubing, Ken Brett, and John Sevano (California Angels); Rob Murphy (Boston Red Sox); Brook Jacoby, Candy Maldonado, Greg Swindell, and Mike Hargrove (Cleveland Indians); Don Mattingly, Pascual Perez, and Bucky Dent (New York Yankees); Rod Carew, Mike Fetters, Bryan Harvey, and Joe Coleman (California Angels); Gregg Olson, Brian Holton, Elrod Hendricks, Al Jackson, and Kathy Case (Baltimore Orioles); Mel Allen and Tony Kubek (New York Yankees); Skip Caray (Atlanta Braves); Bobby Bragan (Texas Rangers); Jolene Murcer; Bud "Steamer" Furillo (KFOX radio); Steve Rosenthal (Westwood One); Jerry Cohen (Ebbets Field Flannel Co.); Ted Tornow (Memphis Chicks); Glenn Geffner (Rochester Red Wings); Kyle Woodell (Rochester Red Wings); Mark Wilson (San Jose Giants); Pamela Gentry (Grand Hyatt on Union Square, San Francisco); Jeff Allen (Hyatt Regency, San Francisco); and all those individuals who turned me down for information on the subject—hey, it's their right, and even some of the turndowns were funny.

I thank the Brea Public Library, Brea, California, for bending the rules and allowing me to check out reference books for well beyond the normal one-month period.

I publicly acknowledge the efforts of all the members of SABR (Society for American Baseball Research) who helped me and showed their funny bones.

I proclaim public recognition to California Angels director of publicity Tim Mead, who showed humor in the face of a trying season and gave in to my whims and whimsy, allowing me to come and go, virtually as I pleased, during the 1990 baseball season in Anaheim, California.

Finally, my thanks to a genuinely funny, odd, and idiosyncratic individual—Richard Topp, the altruistic, accurate, entertaining, and informative president of SABR, who gave me more information than I can print (All-Star list? What list?), more laughs than I deserved, and enough stories to fill another book.

Prologue

A voice came from out of the heavens (or from my publisher, . . . I forget which) and said, "If you write it . . . they will buy it. . . . Go the distance."

So begins this strictly-for-fun-and-information view of baseball, America's pastime, and those bigger-than-life nuances exhibited by those bigger-than-life athletes who fill our sports pages.

This book attempts to provide a Roget's on mannerisms; a Bartlett's on good luck charms; a Webster's on eccentricities; an ALF on baseball superstitions, rituals, oddities, and idiosyncrasies.

Superstitions: Webster's New World Dictionary defines superstition as "Any belief or attitude . . . that is inconsistent with the known laws of science or with what is generally considered as true or rational; any action or practice based on such a belief or attitude." We're not talking of the mundane here. There are no inclusions of the tame or boring instances of players' aversions to stepping on the white lines or not putting a hat on a bed in a hotel room; no oft-told chestnut of not mentioning a no-hitter (except from one broadcaster's perspective) to the pitcher who's in the process of hurling same—especially when 40-foot–high scoreboards ringing the ballpark can give him the same information; no sophomoric wearing of inside-out "rally caps"; no reports of whistling in the hallway, opening umbrellas in the house, or walking under ladders. We are trying to be more sophisticated than that by including charms, voodoo, food, attire, and mannerisms that, conscious, subconscious, or unconscious, are followed meticulously by a player for fear that stopping the routine will result in failure on the ballfield. And to that we'll add, for just a touch of spice, some odd and freakish injuries that befall our most graceful athletes, and some colorful characters who weave fun into the fabric of the game.

Rituals: Somewhat the same as superstitions except that these routines, acts, twitches, and physical celebrations are preconceived and performed with one thing in mind—success.

Oddities: A catch-all myriad of miscellany including offbeat promotions; strange behavior; off-the-wall injuries not usually associated with coordinated celebrity-athletes; weird occurrences, strange deaths, and hard-to-believe events, proving truth is stranger than fiction. And all of the above, which fit within the title of this book, include the ballplayer's friend: idiosyncrasies.

Idiosyncrasies: The neuroses that make the game great.

The best players in the game have them—check out the career stats we've included. The legends use them. The offbeat ones create them. Superstitions, rituals, and oddities may be what make the cream rise to the top.

What is superstitious? or ritualistic? or odd? or idiosyncratic? What is strange or merely just a personal form of mechanics and preparation? Where do they merge with the accomplishments on the diamond? We do not judge, but merely report—for fun. And, as we point out in the pages to follow, in many cases these mysterious machinations achieve the desired effect—wonderful performances in the toughest of arenas, America's pastime.

This book is not in print to hurt anyone, just to have fun with the people who make up this grand old game. Some of what appears here is not superstition per se, but a means of preparation—mental preparation—a way for some of the greatest athletes of sport to attain a degree of greatness that will stand the test of time.

There's a lot of funny stuff here, but in some cases, it is not funny.

Point One: It is preparation—Wade Boggs methodically runs his warm-up laps at precisely 7:17 each night at Fenway Park (see chapter 2) and eats chicken (see chapter 5) before each game with the belief that "there are hits in chicken." Well, Wade Boggs is a career .352 hitter—fourth on the all-time baseball batting list and winner of five AL batting titles. So if Wade Boggs is superstitious or ritualistic, or obsessive-compulsive . . . hey, it works for him, and there are about 500 other Major League players who might want to try it. Would Wade consider ending this routine? He said, "The world won't end if I don't do my laps at 7:17," but . . . if it ain't broke, don't fix it.

Point Two: It is countless players doing the same things over and over and over again because they met with success by innocently doing them once in the past, or those such as Phil Rizzuto (see chapter 1), who wouldn't tempt fate by changing something—gum, in this case—that might end a Yankee winning streak.

Point Three: It is occasionally the unfortunate failure to overcome obsessions, as with Kevin Rhomberg, the king of idiosyncratic superstition. Rhomberg (see chapter 2), a solid Minor League player who hit .383 during his short, three-year career with the Cleveland Indians, was driven out of baseball by his own quirks, neuroses, and manias.

And just ask any ballplayer if he has any superstitions, and he'll immediately say, "No, I don't have any." Ask about rituals, and he'll answer, "No. Not me." Habits or routines? "No. Not a one." As you walk away, he's likely to continue, . . . "Well, there is that thing I do with my gum; and I've worn the same T-shirt under my uniform since Little League; and always sit at the same spot in the dugout and eat the same number of sunflower seeds in odd innings while on the road; and of course, I do hum the theme from *The Natural* as I take my warm-up swings, but other than that, there's nothing."

To fill the pages of this book, I asked hundreds of ballplayers, current and past, their private thoughts on the subject. I conducted interviews with club officials, broadcasters, historians, and journalists and took pages of testimony. Some, like former Dodgers and Angels executive

Buzzie Bavasi, said, "There used to be more superstitions and odd behavior traits than there are today. Players don't need them today . . . they've got guaranteed contracts and aren't looking over their shoulders."

Joe Garagiola, the NBC "Today" anchor, offered, "Hank Greenberg once told me his only superstition was that he had to touch all four bases after hitting a home run."

Skip Caray, Atlanta Braves announcer, said, "The players today are more sophisticated than those of the past, so the draw toward superstition is diminished."

But Bavasi, Caray, and a large majority of those interviewed, admitted that today's players as well as those of the past, will do anything they feel will give them an edge—mental or physical, real or imagined.

These mannerisms, habits, and procedures exist, and to say they don't is to be arcane, blind, and unobservant. Case in point: One former ballplayer (this is the only time in this book in which I don't name names—as I said in a previous paragraph, "This book is not in print to hurt anyone"), who is now a broadcaster-analyst and of the anachronistic old guard—baseball for baseball's sake; take a funny look but don't do anything to hurt the sport—said, "There aren't any superstitions in baseball."

During one pregame conversation at Anaheim Stadium in May 1990, I asked this broadcaster-analyst if during all his time in baseball he had witnessed any out-of-the-ordinary behavior, rituals, or superstitions exhibited by any of his contemporaries. He focused on the word "superstitions." "No," he said. "I've never seen any. There are no superstitions in baseball. The players are too good to be superstitious; they get here on talent."

I reminded him that Wade Boggs feels compelled to run his warm-up laps at 7:17 each night before a ballgame. He countered with, "If Wade Boggs ran his laps at 7:18, he'd still bat .350." I told him that that wasn't the point. Wade *does* run his laps at 7:17 and eats chicken because he believes there are "hits in chicken." Many batters cross themselves, pitchers throw certain pitches in certain orders, and players sit in particular positions in the dugout to effect good luck. He said, "I'm not holding back on ya, Mike, but I've just never seen any of it during my time in baseball."

He was being honest. But how is that possible? I wondered. This man is a baseball analyst, for crying out loud. How can he not see what's going on before his eyes? Does he just love baseball too much, or is he too close to it to see anything detrimental or anything that does not occur between the white lines during the nine innings? Was it just a polite put-down? At least Bob Uecker told me, "I can't really think of any offhand . . . Heck, I wasn't in the game long enough to have any superstitions. I was gone before I could make any up."

The purpose of this book is fun—it is not in print to "out" anyone or to injure or ridicule anyone; it is meant for entertainment and information. But come on, Mr. Broadcaster, and all other diamond jingoists, superstitions exist. Those who are too close to the game, or who deify the game, may fail to realize that baseball, the greatest of all American sports, is made up of men-boys who are no better or worse than any other work group in America. And these men-boys have all the greatness and foibles and strengths and frailties and eccentricities and insecurities as the rest of us. Baseball and baseball players are to be enjoyed, and this book is designed to help the reader do just that—enjoy America's pastime.

Now let's get off the soapbox and have fun.

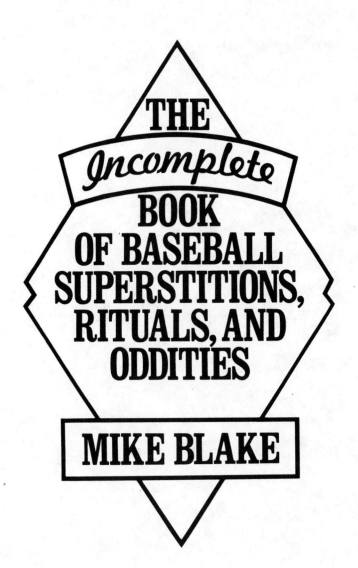

THE Incomplete BOOK OF BASEBALL SUPERSTITIONS, RITUALS, AND ODDITIES

MIKE BLAKE

1
Superstitions

"Superstition," according to John Tyndall, "may be defined as constructive religion which has grown incongruous with intelligence."

While few current ballplayers admit to being superstitious, they and their predecessors have nonetheless openly practiced beliefs and attitudes that show no practical foundation in science or rational society since baseball was conceived by Gen. Alexander Cartwright in 1845 in Hoboken, New Jersey (or Gen. Abner Doubleday, if you must, in 1839 in Cooperstown, New York), about 150 years ago.

Many of these mannerisms, practices, and actions are used as a means of mental preparation, and some are done without explanation. Still others are done "just in case," as baseball players prefer not to tempt fate, looking for any edge they can get to achieve success.

Weird, funny, proper, beautiful, ugly, helpful, nonsensical, and necessary are in the eye of the beholder, but some of what follows, I hope you'll agree, is weird; some is just plain funny; and some simply defies description.

Babe Ruth

George Herman "Babe" Ruth, who makes nearly every chapter of this book—he obviously was a legend in more ways than one—gets mentioned here in a tongue-in-cheek fashion by his old roommate, Jimmy Reese, who is currently a conditioning and fungo coach for the California Angels. In his sixty-first year of Major League ball, Reese estimates that he's hit 1.5 million fungoes over the years, hitting them just within the reach of his targets—Major League fielders.

Ruth, of course, was well known for his hitting prowess, his monstrous home runs, his great left arm (beginning his career as one of the top pitchers in the game), and his on- and off-the-field behavior, but Reese recalls that the man had a great sense of humor with a sprinkling of superstition blended in.

Reese, born James Harrison Solomon, was a diminutive second sacker for the Yankees in 1930 and '31, and the Cardinals in '32. At five feet eleven, 165 pounds, he was no match for the Babe's hulking six-foot-two, 235 pounds (the weight varied, but that would have been a good guess for 1930). And in 1930, when the following incident occurred, Ruth hit .359 with 49 round-trippers, while the rookie Reese batted a credible .346 with three homers.

As Reese tells it, he was rooming with Ruth's luggage— he says Ruth was rarely in his room long enough to be considered a real roommate—and he was in awe of the man.

Before one game, Reese was dressing near the Babe, and as both men started to leave the clubhouse to hit the field, Reese inadvertently stepped in front of Ruth.

Feigning anger, Ruth bellowed, "No one steps in front of me when I go out to the field. That's bad luck. For that, you'll have to go in my locker."

Bewildered, and not 100 percent certain the Bambino was kidding, Reese was at a loss when the bigger Ruth folded him up and placed him in the locker.

Ruth left, and Reese extricated himself and marched out to the field. During the game that followed, Ruth blasted two home runs.

The next day, Reese thought nothing of the previous day's events, and as he started to hit the field, Ruth stopped him.

"You know, Rook," he said, "I put you in the locker yes-

terday and I hit two homers. You can't break the string, so you'll have to go in the locker again."

Before he could protest, Reese was folded up by Ruth and placed in his locker again.

That game, Ruth again connected for two home runs and a double.

On the third day, Reese was resigned to having to spend the rest of his life in Babe Ruth's metal locker. He sighed, and with slumped shoulders, walked over to Babe, fully prepared to be folded up and put away.

Ruth laughed, folded up the infielder, and once again put him in the locker.

The streak continued as Ruth blasted another home run.

Now Reese knew that the locker was to be his home for as long as Babe wanted it that way. Babe was a hero and got anything he wanted, and if Jimmy Reese must spend his career as Babe Ruth's locker totem, then so be it.

On day four, Reese looked into Ruth's eyes. He sighed again and went to the locker willingly. He expected to be folded and shoved into the cubicle again, but Ruth held up his hand and stopped Reese.

Ruth smiled at him and said, "That's OK, Jimmy. You don't need to go in the locker today. All I want to hit is one, and I can do that without any luck."

Reese heaved a sigh of relief and followed Ruth out to the field, where he proceeded to watch the "Sultan of Swat" belt out the one home run he said he wanted to hit.

And the superstitious ritual had ended.

Minnie Minoso

Saturnino Orestes Armas Arrieta Minoso, the flamboyant, Cuban-born outfielder with the sweet swing, is the only man ever to play baseball in five decades—the '40s, '50s, '60s, '70s, and '80s—and may make that six decades this year with a special appearance for the Chicago White Sox. Following a brilliant career in the Cuban League and the Negro National League, Minoso finally was allowed to play in the Major Leagues when he broke in with the Cleveland Indians in 1949 at the age of 27. He has played in 17 seasons and has accumulated a .298 average, 186 home runs, and 1,023 RBIs, despite that late start into "The Show." But the fleet-footed, strong-armed, graceful hitter didn't make this list for his abilities; it is his superstitions and rituals that get him remembered here.

One annual custom was to report late to spring training, though spring training was in Florida, only 90 miles from his native Cuba. His excuses ranged from no room at a hotel, to rain forecast in the area, to no room on the airplanes, to having to do work in the sugar cane fields, but Minnie was always a few days late to camp. Still, that is only habitual, not ritual. What makes Minnie one for the superstition roles is his habit of cleansing away evil slump spirits. Whenever Minoso went into a slump—sometimes that slump consisted of one hitless day—he would run into the clubhouse shower fully clothed and engulf himself in soap and water with his uniform on. "I wash away evil spirits this way," he said. After one clean routine, Minoso connected for three hits the next game, and following the last out, eight of his teammates jumped into the shower fully clothed.

Joaquin Andujar

The veteran right-handed hurler from the Dominican Republic (127–118 in his first 13 seasons), has followed Minoso's lead by showering fully clothed following a poor pitching performance, to wash away the evil spirits that caused his terrible performance. Certainly *he* was not responsible for failing to get opponents out.

Pepper Martin and Ducky Medwick

For some unremembered reason, hairpins have always been considered lucky by ballplayers—especially hitters, who thought that finding a woman's hairpin was a surefire sign that hits and good things would happen. Submerged in a deep slump in 1934 (he finished at only .289), John Leonard Roosevelt "Pepper" Martin of the St. Louis Cardinals hungrily searched around for something that would improve his lot. Martin, also known as "The Wild Hoss of the Osage," played his entire 13-year career (1929–1944) with the Cards and his .298 average indicates that he either didn't need the pins or found a whole passel of them.

Understanding Pepper's superstition, *St. Louis Star-Times* reporter Ray Gillespie and Cardinal shortstop Leo "The Lip" Durocher conspired to give the third baseman–outfielder some help. Before a game, they liberally sprinkled the area around home plate with women's hairpins, knowing Martin was due out of the dugout any moment to take his pregame swings.

Joseph Michael "Ducky" Medwick, a Hall-of-Fame outfielder and teammate of Martin's from 1932 to 1939, and a career .324 hitter over 17 Big League seasons, also believed in the power of the pin, and being hit-hungry (he only hit .319 that year) picked up the pins as fast as he could find them.

As Medwick gobbled up the metal, Durocher and Gillespie shouted to him. "Leave the pins alone; they're for Pepper," they chimed.

As Medwick continued his search along the ground, he looked up at the pair and yelled back, "To hell with Pepper, these hits are mine."

As evidenced by their final stats that year, the pins worked for Medwick, while Martin kept searching . . . for his pins and his hits.

Lou Gehrig and "Shoeless Joe" Jackson

Among others who swore by the luck of and in women's hairpins were Lou Gehrig, the Yankee "Iron Horse" who belted 493 homers and compiled a .340 batting average in 17 seasons, and someone as different from Gehrig as night is from day—except for their quick, strong swings and success on the field—Joseph Jefferson "Shoeless Joe" Jackson, the .356 career hitter for Philadelphia, Cleveland, and Chicago who was thrown out of baseball for his part in the 1919 "Black Sox" scandal.

Gehrig picked up bobby pins whenever and wherever he found them and would play with them (open and close them, pry them apart, and squeeze them together) as he walked along. He never picked up anything else, but he actively searched for these good luck items.

Gehrig was a Columbia University graduate, a New York

born and raised first baseman whose integrity was never questioned; a player who belted 493 homers and stole 102 bases in his career, a masculine man who openly embraced ballet and opera—*Tristan and Isolde* was a favorite opus—and who was a student of the game of baseball and its nuances. Jackson, on the other hand, was a South Carolina born and raised outfielder who was thrown out of the "game" for his part in the World Series fix of 1919 (though he was exonerated in a court of law), an athlete who hit only 54 career homers but stole 202 bases, a Southern macho man who would rather hunt swans than be caught dead at *Swan Lake,* and who just played ball because he did it well, without any analysis or study. But Jackson, too, had a fixation with women's hairpins. He was compulsive about them. If he found one—and he constantly looked for them—he'd be happy for days and his bat would generally reflect his find. But if he came up empty off the field, he'd scour the diamond and even the stands, looking for the bent metal that would set his mind at ease and help him produce another hit.

If it worked for those guys, I wonder if hairpins will raise my softball average?

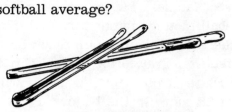

Fred Mitchell

A hairpin saga of another fashion was born in Chicago in the pre-Wrigley days of the 1918 Cubs. Leading his club to a first-place finish (85 wins and 45 losses) was skipper Fred Mitchell.

Mitchell's hairpin superstition went further than hits—it went all the way to wins. Mitchell believed that if he found a hairpin, his team would win.

The Cubs won on one day he happened to find one of the

bent pieces of metal, and for the next 17 days he actively, purposefully searched the grounds, the streets, the stands, and his hotel lobby for hairpins. Miraculously, he found at least one a day for 17 consecutive days, and astonishingly enough, though not to him, the Cubbies proceeded to knock off another 17 straight wins.

On the 19th day of the streak, Mitchell searched for hours but came up empty. Had the Cubs played a night game and he'd had another five hours to search, he might have rewritten history, but the daylight affair made him stop his search short without success.

No hairpin . . . and that meant no victory for the Cubs. The loss returned them to mortal, but the streak was enough to carry them to a National League flag.

Tired of the process, Mitchell didn't go out of his way to find any more pins, but he always felt it a great omen if he happened upon one.

Satchel Paige

Leroy Robert "Satchel" Paige, perhaps the greatest pitcher in baseball history, pitched in the Negro Leagues (for, among others, the Birmingham Black Barons, Cleveland Cubs, Pittsburgh Crawfords, Kansas City Monarchs, and St. Louis Stars) from 1927 to 1950, winning 123 games. He won 28 more in the Majors. Paige also barnstormed around the country pitching in as many as 300 games a year—at age 55, he still took the mound more than 150 times—and probably threw in more than 8,000 games (with 55 no-hitters) over his 40-year career.

Paige was too good to doctor the ball, but he would often engage in head games with opposing hitters. He once told Major League Hall-of-Famer Ducky Medwick he would strike him out on three pitches, and while getting Medwick to wave at each low pitch, he did exactly that. Another time, while pitching for the Pittsburgh Crawfords against the

Homestead Grays, he purposely walked two batters to load the bases for six-foot-two, 217-pound catcher Josh Gibson, "the Babe Ruth of the Black Leagues" (he hit .474 for Homestead in 1943), who is the only man ever to hit a fair ball out of Yankee Stadium. Paige yelled to Gibson to set him up and said, "I'm gonna put these guys on and pitch to you." Before the first pitch to Gibson, Paige yelled, "I'm throwing you a fastball," which he did, and which Gibson took, for strike one. Paige told Gibson another fastball was coming, and the slugger took it for strike two. Paige smiled and nodded at the hitter and whipped an 0–2 fastball at Gibson's knees for strike three, ending the inning.

And while Paige mastered the scam of beginning his windup with his heel against the pitching rubber, coming to a set two feet in front of the pitcher's mark and releasing the ball virtually on top of a hitter, Satchel needed no extra edge to come out a winner . . . except for his superstitions.

One of his favorite beliefs was that if he tied a lucky string bracelet on his wrist, he would win the ballgame, and Satch tied the string and won many times.

On July 30, 1949, while pitching in the Majors for the Cleveland Indians, the 43-year-old hurler was ordered by home plate umpire Bill Summers to remove the string, as it distracted the hitters. Paige protested but untied his lucky bracelet. After pitching a complete game that day, beating the Boston Red Sox 10–6, Paige sauntered to home plate silently, bent down in front of Summers, lifted his pant leg and brought down his stocking, and showed the umpire another lucky string tied around his leg. Paige smiled at Summers and, with a twinkle in his eye, strode away, his lucky charm and self-respect intact.

Phil "The Scooter" Rizzuto

The spark plug for the New York Yankee dynasty from 1941 to 1956 was shortstop Phillip Francis Rizzuto. The

Scooter was also about the most superstitious ballplayer ever to walk onto a diamond. He would always step on second base when going out to his position on the field, purposely drive by a cemetery on the way to a game—for good luck—and chew gum.

Late in 1951, Mickey Mantle's first year and Joe DiMaggio's last, the Bronx Bombers were smack in the middle of a tight pennant race. Rizzuto was having a solid season and nonchalantly popped a new stick of gum in his mouth prior to the next road game. The Yankees won, snapping a short losing streak, and just as Phil was about to toss the worn-out peppermint away, he was reminded by teammates not to do anything to disrupt this new winning streak. Phil agreed, took the gum out of his mouth, and stuck it to the button on top of his baseball cap to save it for the next game.

The following day, Phil took the stale gum off his cap and chewed it—all through the game, which the Yanks won. As the Yankee winning streak reached two weeks—and 11 games—Phil noticed that the gum had begun to smell. It looked odd and tasted worse. Helpful and playful Yankee teammates, aware of the chewy situation, had doctored the gray ball with pepper, linament, and several unspeakable additions. Still, Phil, not wanting to take responsibility for killing a streak, continued on. As the streak reached three weeks and 18 games, Phil gagged as he bravely put this tired old piece of chewed rubber in his mouth. When the first-place pinstripers finally lost game 19, Phil felt down but, with a sense of relief, was finally able to throw the moldy chicle away. Said Phil, "If the Yankees kept winning, I would still be chewing that awful thing today."

[*Author's note:* Other gum chewers who routinely parked their rubbery globs on their cap buttons included **Harold "Prince Hal" Chase,** first baseman for the New York Yankees and four other teams from 1905 to 1919, **Frank Crosetti,** shortstop for the New York Yankees for 17 seasons and a Yankee coach for 20 more, **Eddie Collins,** second baseman for the A's and White Sox for 25 years, and **William "Baby Doll" Jacobsen,** outfielder for the St. Louis Browns and four other teams from 1915 to 1927. Each of these men was a hero of his day—and all were subject to the whims, whimsy, cruelty, prankishness, pepper, and linament of their teammates. Sometimes their gum (and gums) burned like hell, but that seldom swayed their superstitious chewing.]

Bobo Newsom

Louis Norman "Bobo" Newsom, the pitcher who won 211, lost 222, and played for the Dodgers, Cubs, Browns, Senators, Red Sox, Browns again, Tigers, Senators again, Dodgers again, Browns a third time, Senators a third time, A's, Senators a fourth time, Yankees, Giants, Senators a fifth time, and A's again, over a 20-year period, would never tie his own shoelaces. He would dress before each start, stand in the middle of the clubhouse, and wait for someone else to tie his shoes.

Another Newsomism was his fear of paper. He absolutely couldn't stand to see even the tiniest piece of paper cluttering the mound as he was pitching. When he saw any, Newsom would come unglued, stop pitching, and pick up any and all scraps, even if he had to get down on his hands and knees in the middle of a game to police the area.

Knowing this, opponents would routinely throw reams of paper on the field whenever he pitched. If Newsom saw this, a fight could very well ensue.

When Gene Mauch was a 23-year-old utility infielder for the Chicago Cubs, he was talked—read that needled, coerced, or egged on—into tearing up scraps of paper, putting them in his pocket, and scattering them over the mound as he left the field at the end of an inning. Newsom, then pitching for the New York Giants, was to return to pitch the following frame.

According to Mauch, Newsom's rage and nervous behavior ended with the pitcher being tagged for several hits, runs, and a loss.

Other Newsom phobias and superstitions began with touching, with his toe, fair and foul territory as he took the mound; sipping from the water cooler with his face staring straight ahead and his body contorted the same way each time he sipped; and when placing his glove down, carefully setting it face up, with the heel toward home plate and the fingers toward the outfield.

With all this, and a record 17 uniform changes, Bobo lasted 20 years in the Bigs.

John McGraw

John Joseph "Little Napoleon" McGraw, the Hall-of-Fame third baseman–manager for the New York Giants, Baltimore Orioles, and two other teams during a 16-year playing career overlapping a 33-year managerial career, was as superstitious as they come.

Believing the widespread superstition of the day that empty beer barrels were good luck and a surefire precursor to success, McGraw hired a mule team and driver to pull a wagonload of barrels through the old Polo Grounds before the 1905 World Series between his Giants and the Philadelphia A's. The ruse worked, as the Giants took the crown by beating the A's in five games, 4–1.

Occasionally, McGraw would see to it that a few empty beer barrels were rolled through the lobbies of the hotels where his team stayed, if he needed a win that day.

In 1911, a Giant fan named Charles "Victory" Faust accosted McGraw and spun the story that a fortuneteller had told him that the Giants would win the pennant if Faust was allowed to join the team. Too superstitious to doubt the tale, McGraw signed Faust, a lousy pitcher (who only hurled two innings in the Majors), to a contract.

Faust showed up, warmed up with the team, and sat on the bench at home and on the road, as his team won.

Faust stayed with the club for three years—1911, 1912, and 1913 (only in uniform for 1911)—and the Giants won pennants all three years. When Faust died in 1915, the Giants finished last and tailspun for years.

Maybe the fortuneteller was right.

The Salt Lake Trappers

In 1987 the Salt Lake Trappers of the Pioneer League— Class A—an independent team with a pennant on its mind and cleanliness in the back of its book on things to do, won a record 29 games in a row.

During the streak, it has been reported that none of the players washed their socks and some players washed nothing at all, not even themselves. No wonder they kept winning—the other team couldn't get close enough to them to tag them out. And this streak went on through a blazing hot summer, beginning June 25 with a victory in Pocatello, Idaho, over the Giants' Pocatello farm club, and lasting until July 27, when Salt Lake Trappers' water bills finally, mercifully went up with a 7–5 loss to the Billings Mustangs, a Cincinnati Reds affiliate.

[*Author's Note:* The Salt Lake Trappers are owned by Bill Murray, of "Saturday Night Live" fame. Perhaps we can expect a parody film based on a combination of the Trappers' success and the movie *Field of Dreams*, starring Murray and titled: *Team of Dirt.*]

Rabbit Maranville

Richard Topp, President of SABR (Society for American Baseball Research) reported that Hall-of-Famer Walter James "Rabbit" Maranville, the shortstop who campaigned for his election (.258 average, 28 homers in 23 years, and a mediocre .956 fielding percentage) by taking out full-page ads before the voting, wore a cabbage leaf under his baseball cap, both as a good luck charm and to ward off the heat during the dog days of summer. The nickname "Rabbit" apparently had nothing to do with this affinity for cabbage.

Gene Mauch

The "Little General," Gene Mauch, who played as an infielder for nine years—six teams from 1944 to 1957—and managed for 26 years—four teams from 1960 to 1987—tells this one on himself.

While skippering the California Angels, Mauch, who never wore cowboy boots in his life, was on a road trip to Texas when two of his coaches, Bobby Knoop and Larry "Moose" Stubing, talked him into buying some boots. He bought them, but that was as far as he thought it would go.

On the next home stand in Anaheim, Knoop and Stubing talked Mauch into wearing the boots for luck. The Angels were facing Bert Blyleven, who regularly beat them (Blyleven was 28–14 with a 2.45 ERA against his current team), and Mauch thought he'd try anything to help out.

Wearing the boots, the Halos whipped Blyleven and the Twins.

On the Angels' next road trip—to Minnesota to face Blyleven again—Mauch said, "I took the damn things with me."

The magic had worn off, though, and Blyleven got the win over California.

As Mauch threw the losing Western foot-coverings away, he lamented, "You just can't trust cowboy boots." He never wore them again.

Mauch also admits that many players and some managers, himself included, would take strategic routes to the ballpark. The routes would deviate with the success of the team, and a victory was worth taking the same path to the stadium every day until a loss occurred.

Clark Griffith

Clark Calvin "The Old Fox" Griffith was an ace pitcher who manned the mound for the Chicago Cubs, Chicago White Sox, Yankees, Senators, and three other clubs from 1891 to 1914. The five-foot-six, 156-pound Hall-of-Famer won 240 games over 21 years but wound up with only 23 shutouts in nearly 400 starts.

As a pitcher, it was his duty to record outs and refrain from allowing runs, yet this man's superstitions superceded that obligation. While he would never intentionally put a game in jeopardy or lose a game, he did occasionally prefer to give up runs rather than induce outs.

Griffith's superstition was that he thought shutouts were more than bad luck—he felt they were a sin. A deeply religious man, he believed that shutting out his fellow man was disgracing him, and to purposely disgrace a fellow human being was to bring shame in the eyes of the Lord.

With a 1–0 lead, he could live with the shame, but up 3–0 or 4–0, he felt it was better to give than to receive, and he gave up runs as an offering to his deity.

Bob Boyd

From Ernie Harwell, the "Voice of the Detroit Tigers," comes this story about Bob "The Rope" Boyd, the strong-armed, good-hitting (.292 career) Baltimore Orioles first baseman–outfielder from 1956 to 1960. Boyd used to keep a rope in the pocket of his baseball uniform. At several points during each game, he would reach in and hold his rope. Boyd's reasoning was that this would allow him to hit "ropes," or line drives, and also throw balls back into the infield on a "rope" or line. The tag line to this superstition is that one day it backfired. During a game against the Indians in Cleveland, Boyd fielded a ball on a few hops and fired the sphere back to home in an effort to nail an Indian runner who was trying to score. The run scored and Boyd snapped his arm on the throw, breaking it and keeping him out of action for a month. The rope broke and so did Boyd.

Moe Berg

How does one describe a ballplayer who graduated from Princeton University; spoke 12 languages; was an adequate shortstop who became a catcher when other catchers on his team fell ill, and then made himself into one of the best defensive pitcher-handlers of his time; gained knowledge of nuclear physics and worked on the Manhattan Project; was employed by the OSS (the forerunner to America's CIA) and parachuted behind enemy lines during World War II to kidnap German, Italian, and Scandinavian atomic scientists to aid the United States in its war effort; and who nearly always wore black? While the description might come down to "enigmatic," the aforementioned information would fill but a brief dossier on Morris "Moe" Berg.

As a player, Berg lasted 15 years, playing from 1923 to 1939 with the Brooklyn Dodgers, Chicago White Sox, Washington Senators, Boston Red Sox, and Cleveland Indians, batting .243—the joke of the day was that Berg could speak 12 languages and couldn't hit in any of them—and compiling a .986 fielding percentage behind the plate.

He didn't drink or smoke, but he did have quirks. A voracious reader, he never read a newspaper if anyone else had read it or even touched it. He said that virgin newspapers were "alive" and used newspapers were "dead." He would walk miles through storms and snow to buy a "live" paper. "When a newspaper's dead," Berg would say, "you can't read it."

He also brought books with him to the bull pen and, during the games, read them until he had to warm someone up. Reading, he thought, was good for the mind, and good luck. As long as he read, he reasoned, the starter would pitch well enough to stay in. When he stopped reading, it meant relief help was needed.

Berg was perhaps the only player in baseball history to always keep a pressed tuxedo in his locker. "Just in case," he said.

And whenever anyone talked to him, Berg would take napkins and scribble notes on them. The notes were usually written in Sanskrit or some foreign language that looked like senseless scribblings to others.

Without fail, after playing a full game behind the plate, Berg would refrain from joining his teammates in alcoholic revelry, saying, "I've got to rest the body . . . rest the body."

Though not a superstition and more of an odd behavioral exhibition, on one occasion, to protest stall techniques employed by his own pitcher, Earl Whitehill of the Washington Senators, and the hitter, Doc Cramer of the Philadelphia A's, Berg stripped off all of his catching gear and piled it on home plate. He explained to bewildered umpire Bill McGowan, "When these guys are ready to play baseball, call me. Right now, I'm going to take a shower."

Berg's final superstition dealt with food or, as he called it, "fuel." "Have to fuel the body," said Berg. The catcher was apparently years ahead of his time, as he daily swore by raw and smoked fish—usually in the forms of lox, or smoked salmon, and sushi, or raw tuna and other fresh fish. The love of lox may have come from Berg's ethnic heritage, and the sushi may have come from Berg's trip to Japan with the American All-Stars in 1934—a trip on which Berg took spy photos of Japanese installations, photos which were used during the Jimmy Doolittle raids over Tokyo 10 years later.

Whatever the reason, Berg's eating habits were thought to be odd in the '30s, but are *très chic* today. Hey, the man does lox and sushi. He's hip.

Rogers Hornsby

Not quite as determined or as scholarly as Berg was Rogers Hornsby, the .358-career batting phenom for the St. Louis Cardinals and Chicago Cubs. Hornsby merely refused to read newspapers at all. He said, "They're bad for the eyes." And with 2,930 hits over 23 years, and an average more than 100 points higher than Berg's, "The Rajah's" eyes and eyesight were never questioned.

Monkey Hotaling

Peter James "Monkey" Hotaling, a fleet-footed (43 stolen bases in 1887 for the Cleveland Blues) five-foot-eight, 166-pound center fielder for seven teams in the National League and American Association from 1879 to 1888 (he committed 264 errors in 840 games), lived up to his nickname by keeping a monkey's paw by his side at all times. It apparently didn't work too well in the field.

"Foghorn Dick" Van Zant

There's no evidence to indicate that Richard "Foghorn Dick" Van Zant, a part-time third baseman for the 1888 Cleveland Blues of the American Association, followed "Monkey's" lead by being true to his own nickname and keeping a small foghorn in his pocket, but he did hold onto another keepsake for luck—a pig's ear, which he bought from an Indiana farmer. The story has been told that a young Van Zant was escaping from a girl's father—in a

"Farmer's Daughter" routine—following a juvenile tryst, when he was attacked by pigs. He came away with cuts and scrapes, and the porcine stampede apparently kept the farmer-father and his shotgun at bay. From that day on, Foghorn thought pigs to be lucky, though the particular ear he collected was hardly good luck to its original owner.

Jim Toy

James Madison Toy, reputed to be the first Native American (American Indian) to play Major League baseball (1887 with the Cleveland Blues and 1890 with the Brooklyn Gladiators), was a utility ballplayer who filled in at first base, shortstop, third base, catcher, and the outfield over 153 games while batting an anemic .211. His superstitions, though common to his culture, were looked at with a jaundiced eye by those relatively unsophisticated ballplaying contemporaries of the day.

Toy carried around beads, small totems, pipes, charms, fetishes, and talismans associated with his Native American religious practices, but to skeptical, uneducated ballplayers of the late 1800s, if it wasn't a rabbit's foot, it was considered weird.

Toy also was "one with nature" and would employ a form of meditation quite often before playing ball. This, too, was an uncommon occurrence during that era and was thought to be odd.

Whether Toy carried out his practices for luck, superstition, or strict religious belief is not clear, but as it was not the run-of-the-mill behavior of the age, it is included here.

Skip Caray

The entertaining announcer for the Atlanta Braves, Skip Caray, speaks of the oft-told superstition of never mentioning a no-hitter. This rule is routinely broken—first, perhaps, by Red Barber; lately, by nearly every non-superstitious broadcaster—and Caray admits he caught flack when he chose to clue the listeners in to what was happening on the field. Andy Messersmith was tossing a no-no for the Atlanta Braves against the Montreal Expos, and Caray kept reporting same. According to Caray, "The fan wants to know what's going on, and late-listening fans deserve to find out exactly what is taking place . . . so he won't change stations or go on to something else. It is our job to mention it. I told the audience, as we entered the seventh inning, that Messersmith was nine outs away from completing a no-hitter, and almost immediately, Andy gave up a base hit. I got angry phone calls and letters for weeks criticizing me, my family, and ability as a broadcaster for 'blowing' the no-hitter." Caray sums up his feelings on the situation by saying, "Nobody, as a group, has more ego than announcers, but not even we think we have any control over anything that happens on the field . . . particularly by what we say."

Willie Mays

Willie Mays, the ex-Giant Hall-of-Famer who is often said to possess the greatest skill the game has ever seen, needed no luck to help him accomplish his 3,283 hits, 660 home runs, 1,903 RBIs, and .302 career marks. But Mays made sure, for luck, that he touched second base on his way to or from the outfield every inning.

And remember the vision of fleet-footed Willie running out from under his cap as he literally flew around the bases and around the outfield? Mays was superstitious—or self-conscious—about appearing slow, so he purposely wore a hat that was one size too large—it would fly off and make him look faster. Mays admitted as much only after he retired.

Walter Johnson and Alvin Crowder

Another good-luck tale Ernie Harwell likes to relate deals with Hall-of-Fame pitcher Walter "Big Train" Johnson and rookie hurler Alvin "General" Crowder.

Walter Johnson was a hard-throwing (estimated 100-mph fastball) right-hander for the Washington Senators who won 416 games and struck out 3,508 hitters (a record that stood for more than 55 years until Nolan Ryan broke it on April 27, 1983, by whiffing Brad Mills of Montreal) between 1907 and 1927. He had just won his 400th game when a 1926 teammate, a brash, cocky rookie from North Carolina named Alvin Crowder, who won 167 games and struck out 799 between 1926 and 1936 (playing for four teams), came up to him and asked to borrow his glove. Crowder, apparently thinking that the 400 wins came from Johnson's glove and not his arm, wanted to pitch with the Big Train's leather.

Johnson readily gave up the glove, and the rookie won five straight games (he won only seven all season).

When the 26-year-old rookie finally lost, in that sixth game, he threw the five fingers of leather back at Johnson and said, "You can take this thing back . . . it's bad luck." By the middle of the next year, Crowder had been peddled to the St. Louis Browns, finishing his second consecutive seven-win season.

Leo "The Lip" Durocher

In the 1954 World Series, New York Giants manager Leo Durocher chose to start outfielder Monte Irvin every game, then replace him with pinch hitter James Lamar "Dusty" Rhodes when there was someone on base ahead of Irvin. He did it for luck, and the move worked, as Rhodes was the hero of games two and three in the Giant sweep of Cleveland. Rhodes went 4-for-6 with seven RBIs and Irvin went 2-for-9 with 2 RBIs. During the season, Rhodes hit .341 in 82 games, while Irvin hit .262 in 135 games, but still Durocher chose to start Irvin and go with Rhodes in a strategic situation (for luck) later.

Ross Grimsley

Ross Grimsley was a lefty hurler who went 124–99 over an 11-year career for Cincinnati, Baltimore, Montreal, and Cleveland. He showed some brilliance, but at times he literally "stunk"—due, in part, to his superstition.

Grimsley felt compelled to refrain from washing, combing his hair, or using deodorant while he was winning. He wouldn't cleanse himself, comb, or do anything that might wash away his good fortune.

His teammates threatened to lose on purpose just to inflict hygiene on him. The unclean Grimsley, while winning, tooled around town, smelly, shirtless, wearing torn jeans and scruffy sandals—a great character model for young baseball fans everywhere.

Called "Skuz" by his teammates, Grimsley was said to "moon" carloads of women by exposing his unwashed derriere from moving vehicles, and the unwashed hurler was also known to "streak"—run naked—through hotels as a source of self-amusement.

Vida Blue

Vida Blue, the lefty who was done too soon—he lasted 17 years and won 201 games for Oakland, San Francisco, and Kansas City, but he lost several years due to injury and off-the-field transgressions—believed that good luck was imbedded in the baseball cap he had worn since the first game of 1974. He wore it for three complete seasons, winning 17, 22, and 18 games in those years.

Blue attempted to wear the stained, dirty, sweaty, and faded A's cap in 1977, and umpires threatened to throw him out of the game. He protested and was told to get it off or get out. He complied, but not before he burned the cap in a pregame good-luck ceremony on the field. With the lucky hat in flames, Blue went on to lead the league—in losses, with 19.

Roger Craig and the Dirt of Dreams

In early June of 1990, the San Francisco Giants were floundering in the National League West. Unexpectedly, Giants' manager Roger Craig, a veteran of 12 Big League seasons as a player (pitcher) and eight seasons and more than 1,000 games at the helm of the Padres and Giants, received an unsolicited package in the mail.

The gift was a small plastic capsule filled with dirt. But not just any dirt—the earth had been sent by a Giants fan, a woman who had just visited the Iowa ballfield-cornfield where the movie *Field of Dreams* had been filmed.

A letter, enclosed with the plastic vial, told Craig that the dirt had been scooped up from the pitcher's mound in Dyersville, Iowa, and that keeping it would help the Giants attain their dreams.

Craig kept the dirt with him, and the Giants won 15 of their next 16 games and made a race of it in the NL West.

Craig also makes the superstitions list for an act of defiance he committed in 1962. While pitching for the '62 New York Mets, arguably the worst team in baseball history, Craig had lost 15 straight games en route to a 10–24 season. He decided to try to stop the streak by changing his uniform number for one game. He chose number 13. Good choice.

The result: Craig lost that game also, by a romp of 15–2.

Rod Carew

Rod Carew, arguably baseball's top hitter for 19 years, from 1967 to 1985, during which time he won seven batting titles en route to a .328 career mark and 3,053 hits, had one superstition that didn't escape Gene Mauch. Mauch said, "Whenever Carew went 0-for-2 in a game, which wasn't that often, or if he went 0-for-1 but looked bad doing it, he would take off the pair of baseball shoes he'd been wearing and put on a new pair."

The outs were in the shoes.

Carew denied that he had a routine of filling his mouth with gum and/or tobacco in order to create a perfect line of sight from his eye, across the line of his bulging cheek, to the pitcher's throwing hand. He claimed that that was a media fabrication. But he did maintain that he had another superstition. He said, "I made it a point never to talk to writers after batting practice." While that sounds flip, Carew explained that he used the time to mentally prepare for the game at hand and didn't want to be distracted.

OK, so I didn't take it personally.

Gene Mauch, the much-traveled, highly regarded manager, related the following superstitions of those with or against whom he played:

Veteran players must sometimes concentrate as much as is humanly possible to get a few more good games out of their aging bodies, and **Don Hoak,** an 11-year National League infielder for five teams, had to meditate late in his career to be successful on the field. Mauch said, "Hoak used to think of a guy on the other team who he hated and really work up a frenzy to beat that particular guy. That provided his motivation."

Andy Cohen, a coach Mauch had with the Phillies in 1960 (Cohen played the infield for three years with the New York Giants some 30 years earlier and held a long career as a coach) and a man who managed Mauch at Denver in the American Association, used to go over to the corner of the coach's box and bow to the east before each game—something not usually associated with men of Cohen's Jewish faith. Cohen never explained the significance of the ritual, but it was understood he did it for luck.

A story from ex-Dodger hurler Joe Black, a 15–4 Rookie of the Year for the Brooklyn Dodgers in 1952, tells of the time **Carl Erskine** no-hit the Chicago Cubs, June 19, 1952, and the team not only broke with tradition by mentioning it early on, but teammate **Dick Williams** began doing a "play by play" in the dugout as early as the third inning. With a perfect inning completed, the dugout Dodgers demanded Williams play broadcaster again in the fourth . . . and fifth . . . and sixth.

By then, Williams's throat was tired, but he continued to make like Red Barber as he led Erskine through the seventh and eighth.

The Dodgers in the dugout hung on his every word. They demanded that the now-hoarse utility infielder-outfielder continue rather than break the lucky string. Williams went on until he was able to say, "It's all over. Carl Erskine has pitched a no-hitter."

Also from Black comes the story that **Charley "Chuck" Dressen,** Dodger manager from 1951 to 1953, thought it superstitiously bad luck, when he coached third base, if anyone crossed in front of him as he went out to the box. One day **Billy Loes,** Dodger hurler, inadvertently stepped in front of his manager, and Dressen punched him. Down went Loes, but he understood, and never crossed his skipper again.

Old, Dirty Clothes—Fresh, Clean Luck

During a 16-game hitting streak in 1988, Atlanta Braves outfielder **Dion James** did not wash his underwear. He didn't want the good luck to wash out, and he wore the same stale garments in each game. He may have figured that the ball wanted to get as far away from him as possible. The streak eventually ended, and so did James's batting heroics. He finished the year at .256, and by the middle of the next season, a clean, Downy-fresh James was traded to Cleveland, where his average soared from .259 to .306. Maybe Cleveland's water was better for James's underwear than was Atlanta's.

Brook Jacoby, third baseman for the Cleveland Indians, has a favorite shirt he has worn since his rookie season. He wears it under his uniform and has not washed it in years. His All-Star season makes it a pretty safe bet that his superstition is stronger than dirt.

New York Yankee left-hander **Ron "Gator" "Louisiana Lightning" Guidry** was a three-time 20-game winner, and until his retirement from ball in 1988, he wore the same stirrup socks he had worn when he won his first game in 1977.

His teammate, reliever **Dave "Rags" Righetti,** who in 1986 set the Major League record for saves with 46 (since broken by Bobby Thigpen), wears the same black T-shirt he wore during his first win in 1981. He says, "Don't change. Whatever got us here, stays here."

Hall-of-Fame right-hander **Don Drysdale,** a career-long Dodger, wore the same clothes to every game in which he was going to pitch, and the same shorts, undershirt, and cap while pitching. Though he washed the clothes between needed appearances, Drysdale, who won 209 games, said, "It worked. Well, it worked 209 times, anyway."

Dennis "Oil Can" Boyd, now with the Montreal Expos, wore the same warm-up jacket during his entire stay with the Boston Red Sox, from 1982 to 1989, and his teammate **Roger Clemens** still wears the same warm-up jacket he wore during his first win in 1984.

Bryan Harvey, the relief pitcher for the California Angels, who sported a 13–10 career mark through his first three-and-a-half seasons, covering 150 appearances, does not change his clothes until he loses. Presumably that means he wears the same clothes, washed at regular intervals, to the ballpark, as he doesn't get enough decisions to make that sort of arrangement palatable to his more fragrant teammates.

Cincinnati Reds manager **Bill "The Deacon" McKechnie** led his team to a pennant in 1940. To help the team win, he wore the same tie—an old, dirty, stained, spotted rag—every single day. He slept with it, ate with it, wore it to the park, and held it close when he needed it. He and many of his players credit the cloth with providing the edge they needed to win the pennant. The '40 Reds went 100–53, winning more games than any other team during McKechnie's 25 years as a skipper. In '41, he changed ties and the Reds slumped to third place and an 88–66 finish. He must have wondered, "Now, where did I put that thing?"

California Angels manager **Doug Rader** said, "I am not in favor of unhygienic superstitions, but I see no reason why a player or a certain manager [wink] can't come to the park the same way every day . . . as long as we're winning, then begin a new route following a loss."

Other clothing optional decisions:

Ewell "The Whip" Blackwell, the big, six-foot-six right-hander for the Cincinnati Reds (22–8 in 1947), had two sweatshirts—a red one and a white one. Red was thought, during Blackwell's day, to be lucky, but he thought whichever shirt was "hot" was lucky. So he'd wear a shirt until he lost . . . then wear the other one until he lost again. He once made nine straight starts in red before switching to white.

Bob Shawkey, the steady Yankee hurler—four-time 20-game winner, with 196 wins over a 15-year career—was another who wore the lucky red sweatshirt under his uni. He was allowed to continue the practice despite the fact that most other Yankees wore blue or white.

Sal "The Barber" Maglie, the 10-year Major Leaguer who gained his reputation for shaving the batters with his high, hard fastball during a seven-year stint with the New York Giants (a .657 lifetime winning percentage), was a pitcher who always wore sleeves—those long-sleeved undershirts—except on the day he pitched. Pitching bare-armed, regardless of the weather, he said, improved his arm movement and his chances for winning.

Jim Fregosi, California Angels manager from 1978 to 1981, wore his hot, dark blue, fleece-lined warm-up jacket over his uniform every game, all for luck. On days that reached 100 degrees, he looked hot but managed to keep his cool without giving in. His teams finished third, first, sixth, and fourth, and when he moved on to manage the ChiSox in 1987, he brought his hot habit and two fifth-place finishes with him. Maybe he'd be better off if he were comfortable.

Getting out of uniforms and into three quickies . . .

Hugh Casey, the righty hurler for the Brooklyn Dodgers (15–10 in 1939 and a .641 lifetime winning percentage in nine years); **Vic "The Springfield Rifle" Raschi,** who threw for the Yankees (132 wins and 66 losses, three straight 20-win seasons over a 10-year career); and **Charles "Chief" Bender,** the Hall-of-Fame Philadelphia A's right-hander with a 210–127 record in 16 years, all thought photographs before a game amounted to bad luck, and would allow no photographer to get close to them as game time approached.

Bender went so far as to smash several cameras being used by photogs as they ventured near the hurler. No Kodak "memories" commercial for him.

Walt "Moose" Moryn, an outfielder for the Chicago Cubs and others from 1954 to 1961 (101 homers in 785 games, including 26 in 1958) wore a rabbit's foot on his spikes. It must have been unnerving when he ran and fielded, but he kept up the routine.

And **Russ Christopher,** the tall, thin (six-feet-three, 170 pounds) Philadelphia A's pitcher who won 54 and saved 35 during a seven-year career, was known to break slumps by either wearing a straw hat, or carrying keys and good luck charms on his person at all times—even during the ballgames. Judging by his lifetime winning total (10 games under .500), he didn't break enough slumps.

Chief Noc-A-Homa and the 1982 Atlanta Braves

The 1982 Atlanta Braves, led by Dale Murphy, Bob Horner, Claudell Washington, Chris Chambliss, and Phil Niekro, won the first 13 games of the season and streaked to a big lead in the National League West, while their mascot, Chief Noc-A-Homa, danced and pranced in left field after each home run, during each rally, and following each Braves win.

On July 30, 1982, the Braves, in first place in the NL West, with a 10½-game lead, evicted their popular Indian mascot from his teepee in left field, to make room for new seats. The Braves' management knew this would be a pennant year and wanted to make the most of it by enabling more paying patrons to see the team. Besides, they thought, Chief Noc-A-Homa was fun to watch but not crucial to the success or profit of the team.

Wrong.

Immediately following the Chief's removal, the Braves went into a tailspin and lost 19 of their next 21 games, blowing the huge advantage.

Bowing to public pressure, Braves management brought the lucky chief and his teepee back, and the Braves recovered to win the NL West flag.

1990 Boston Red Sox Exorcism

The 1990 Boston Red Sox were locked in a death struggle for the American League East flag with their neighbors to the north, the Toronto Blue Jays, when, in mid-

July, they lost the batting, fielding, and pitching prowess that had put them in first place and withered during the warm summer with 14 losses in 19 games.

Unwilling to stand idly by and let the pennant slip from their grasp, the BoSox decided to perform an exorcism to rid themselves of the evil that had sapped their ability to win.

On July 23, the team erected a voodoo shrine in its clubhouse.

In a ritual featuring 69 candles, a number 13 jersey, two black cats, assorted rubber spiders and snakes, a rooster, chanting and singing, the Bostonians tried to breathe life into slumping bats.

The following game saw the Red Sox score five runs on 11 hits in a 6–5, 11-inning loss to the Milwaukee Brewers, but the 5–15 slide ended the next night when Roger

Clemens won his 13th game as he shut out the Brewers on three hits, 2–0 (the Red Sox collected seven hits).

Give me a ritualistic ceremony and a hot right-handed fireballer, anytime—even one who hasn't changed warm-up jackets in seven years.

[*Author's note:* Clemens wore a ritualistic patch on his sleeve that night that read: "N300R." It was a tribute to fellow Texan Nolan Ryan's quest (unsuccessful that night) to win his 300th game.]

The Number 13

The number 13 is considered by many the world over to be an unlucky one, and most teams have never had anyone wear that albatross. However, it does sneak through sometimes . . . with varied amounts of success. Among those who wore number 13, and didn't consider it unlucky, were **Ralph Branca** (Brooklyn Dodgers, 88 wins in 12 years), who posed with black cats; **Davey Concepcion** (Cincinnati Reds), who invented and perfected the "Astroturf one-hop throw" from short to first; and **John "Blue Moon" Odom** (Kansas City-Oakland A's, 84 wins), who played for 13 seasons in the Majors.

Sporting the number 13 in 1990 were **Ozzie Guillen,** the graceful, funny (see chapter 7), hot-hitting Chicago White Sox shortstop; **Bill Wilkerson,** lefty pitcher for the Kansas City Royals; **Lance Parrish** (Tina Turner's former bodyguard) of the California Angels; **Alvaro Espinoza** who, against odds, weathered the year for the New York Yankees; **Omar Vizquel,** an infielder for the Seattle Mariners; **Roger McDowell,** the enigmatic reliever for the Philadelphia Phillies; second baseman **Jose Lind** of the Pittsburgh Pirates; **Mike Pagliarulo,** third baseman for the San Diego Padres, who used to wear a garter (see p. 52); and **Ernie Camacho,** reliever, San Francisco Giants, who also makes this book (see chapter 6).

Other uniform peculiarities include the 1916 Brooklyn Dodgers, who wore checkered uniforms—with pin-striped squares all over the things that made them look like clowns. The uniforms lasted one year as players' and fans' complaints outweighed the team's first-place finish at 94–60.

Andy Messersmith

Though not a superstition, Andy Messersmith's uniform number 17 deserves recognition. While with the Atlanta Braves in 1976, Messersmith, a talented pitcher for four teams from 1968 to 1979 (for whom he won 130 while losing only 99 and compiling a classy 2.86 ERA), was signed as a free agent and given the number 17 by team owner Ted Turner, who just happened to own television station number 17. Turner then issued Messersmith a new nickname, "Channel," so that "Channel 17" appeared on his back, plugging Turner's station. The National League ordered Turner and Messersmith to cease this walking advertisement, and soon Messersmith got his own name back on his back.

Carlos May

One move to "17" that did work was the choice of Carlos May, a .274 hitter in 10 years as an outfielder-dh for the Chicago White Sox, New York Yankees, and California Angels. May, born May 17, 1948, wore his birthdate on his back. His uniform read "May 17."

Mike Pagliarulo

Mike "Pags" Pagliarulo, the third baseman for the New York Yankees and San Diego Padres who has been on the Major League scene since 1984, has been trying to rid himself of superstitions. Beginning during his days at the University of Miami, Florida, in the late 1970s, he wore a red ribbon attached to his jockstrap. Pags said, "My grandmother gave it to me . . . it's an old Italian custom. Brides wear red ribbons under their dresses for good luck."

He also wore the Italian horn, or *maluckya,* but ceased the practice a few years ago. To fight superstition, he traded in his number 6 pin-striped New York uniform for number 13, which he still wears on his pin-striped San Diego uni. He gave up superstitions so he "wouldn't have anything to blame a bad performance on. They're crutches."

Fact: At the height of his superstitions, Pagliarulo belted 28 homers in 1986 and 32 homers in 1987. Since he discarded his "ritualistic crutches," he has fallen to 15 homers and 7 homers, and 1990 was looming as a single-digit home run year as well.

One wonders if Pags would benefit from a shiny new red ribbon, an Italian horn, and a different number.

Are these superstitions odder than your own? Are you in the Major Leagues? It worked for these guys. Can you say unwashed uniform? I thought you could. Now just pick a number, find a hairpin and an empty beer barrel, and rechew that gum you left on your baseball cap button last week, and you, too, can join "The Show," as a Major League baseball player.

2
Rituals

Webster's New World Dictionary defines rituals as a set form of ceremonies or formal, solemn acts, observances or procedures in accordance with prescribed rule or custom . . . especially at regular intervals.

Some of what follows may not be formal or solemn, but it's all prescribed by custom, at least in the minds of those players performing these acts as another means of mentally preparing for the task at hand—on the field—or as a means of coercing Lady Luck into their dugouts and out of the dugouts of their opponents.

Kevin Rhomberg

Kevin Jay Rhomberg was a good-looking, speedy, great-hitting six-foot, 175-pound outfielder for the Cleveland Indians from 1982 to 1984.

He was a "can't miss" prospect of whom it was said, "The kid can hit. He can hit when he gets out of bed in the morning, and he can hit when he's asleep at night."

Rhomberg proved it too. In 1981, playing AA ball with the Chattanooga Lookouts, he tore the cover off the ball, batting a whopping .367, getting 187 hits in 509 at bats, with 17 triples and 76 stolen bases. He was hitting .400 with less than two weeks left to play before slumping.

As a 27-year-old rookie in 1982, he hit .333 in 12 games and followed that up with a mighty .476 in 1983 and .250

in 1984 during short stints with the Tribe. For his career: a .383 average, only one error in the field, and only 41 games in the Majors. But at the age of 30, he was out of baseball. Why?

Rituals. Or call them quirks or neuroses. Whatever they were, they got the best of Kevin Rhomberg, and he never was able to fulfill his promise.

As early as his Minor League career, players knew Rhomberg could be had.

Game number one, "Touchbacks." This ritual involved always touching someone back who had touched him—a takeoff on the kid's game "Tag, I'll tag you back." But Rhomberg carried it to an extreme. He was obsessed with making that last touch.

Rhomberg said, "It started as a game with my brothers and sisters. Once a guy touched me 118 times, and I got him back every time."

Knowing this, two opposing players with the Savannah Braves of the Southern League, Milt Thompson and Brook Jacoby, decided to have fun with Rhomberg.

According to Jacoby, "We walked up to Rhomberg to have a conversation with him, and we said we knew he had to touch whomever or whatever touched him last. With that we produced a baseball and touched him with it. We told him that now, he had to touch the baseball back."

Jacoby then proceeded to throw the baseball out of the park and into a vacant field near the stadium. He said Rhomberg went after it and spent two hours searching before he found the offending ball.

Tagbacks got out of hand.

"Once," Rhomberg said, "I had to touch the whole opposing pitching staff because I didn't know who touched me. Another time I touched a whole busload of people to make sure I got the right person. Rod Carew touched me once and ran away. I couldn't get him back . . . he was too fast."

Rhomberg explained the compulsion, "My rules, my game, my mind, I win."

Game number two, "At Bat." Before every turn at the plate, Rhomberg would do things in numbers of four: four squirts of water at the water cooler before he left the dugout, four taps of the bat on the ground, four taps of the bat on his helmet, four taps of his cleats with his bat, a left turn into the batter's box, and four practice swings.

Said Rhomberg, "It started when I went four-for-four one day, and I've had success with it ever since. Then the press got ahold of it and leaked it to the public. Then opposing players would interrupt my routine. But it was my game, my mind, my rules, I win."

Game number three, "No Right Turns." Rhomberg would refuse to turn right. Ever. When he stepped out of an elevator, he'd always turn left. If his room was to the right, he'd turn a complete circle going to his left, until he could make his room. On the base paths he was fine—you only make left turns when you run from base to base—but if he was in a rundown, he'd have to circle before going back to a previous base.

Said Rhomberg, "It got so I wouldn't make right turns anywhere. I could always backpedal or turn left and come around in the field. I never had to go right. I did it as a concentration factor and it worked. I always hit around .300 and was a good outfielder. I didn't care what people thought. Then the press got ahold of it and I quit so my children wouldn't have to read that 'Daddy is crazy.'"

But Rhomberg always felt he was a winner, and as he said before, he always won his ritualistic mind games because it was "my rules, my game, my mind, I win." He simply got out of the game because, as he said, "My superstitions and rituals just stopped being fun anymore."

Ed Walsh

Hall-of-Famer Edward Augustine "Big Ed" Walsh was a six-foot-one, 193-pound right-handed hurler for the Chicago White Sox from 1904 to 1916, finishing up his career with the Boston Red Sox in 1917. During the first nine years of his career, Walsh won 182 games—40 in 1908 and 27 each in 1911 and 1912. From 1913 to 1917, though, Walsh managed only 13 more wins, total. What happened? Did he lose his arm? No. He apparently lost his good luck ritual, his sneak pitch, his confidence, and his career, due to a manager and a horse.

Ed Walsh was perhaps the greatest spitball pitcher (a legal pitch at the time) of his day. Hall-of-Fame slugger "Wahoo Sam" Crawford said of Walsh's spitter, "I think the ball disintegrated on the way to the plate and the catcher put it back together again. I swear, when it went by the plate, it was just the spit that went by."

Tall, strong, and good-looking, Walsh, an ex-coal miner, as part of his pitching mechanics, would look in to the catcher, rub the baseball against his tongue and lower lip, lick the sphere, go into his motion, and throw a dipping, tailing, darting pill past the opposing hitter.

Early in 1913, the White Sox ventured into Philadelphia to play a four-game series against the first-place A's, managed by crafty Connie Mack. Mack, the venerable skipper who managed for 53 years (50 consecutive years with the Philadelphia A's) and won 3,731 games and nine pennants, was, as usual, attired in a dark business suit and straw hat. He was tired of losing 1–0 games to Walsh, and he noticed the pitcher's ball-licking routine. He ordered his ballboy to go across the street to some stables near the ballpark and pick up a bucketful of horse droppings.

Upon receiving the manure, the skeletal-like Mack rubbed down all the balls (the home team supplies the baseballs to be used in each game) with the waste material.

Once the game started, Walsh, on the hill, began to lick the excrement-encrusted spheres. He winced, shuddered, and threw up. By the third inning, Walsh had gotten sicker—and the A's shellacked him for eight runs.

Three days later, Walsh was on the mound again, and again got pasted by the A's, who had doctored the balls.

Soon, word spread around the league, and manure was the order of the day. As a result of aversion therapy—each time Walsh licked, he vomited—he soon became unable to put his lips to a ball. He soon lost his rhythm, mechanics, and spitball, and was transformed from franchise-leading winner to run-of-the-mill loser.

All thanks to Connie Mack and the horse he rode in on.

Wade Boggs

Wade Boggs, the classic hitter from Fenway, may some-day have an entire book devoted to his means of mentally preparing for a game (see chapters 5 and 6). While in the on-deck circle, he always puts pine tar, resin, and a weight donut on his bat, in that order, and draws a precise figure in the dirt when he arrives in the batter's box.

But Boggs's most enduring ritual has to be his daily routine of running wind sprints at exactly 3 P.M., first batting practice swings at 6:56, and wind sprints or laps at precisely 7:17 every night.

Said Boggs, "I am naturally time-oriented, and while I know the world won't come to an end if I don't run at 7:17, I see no reason to change what I am comfortable with." He said he looks at the clock and visualizes 7:17 as 7-for-7, a perfect day at the plate and a positive sign.

Gene Mauch pixieishly remembers that one night at Ana-heim Stadium, while he was managing the California An-gels, the Red Sox came to town and Mauch decided to foil the BoSox third baseman. He conspired with the score-board operator, and when the clock struck 7:15 and Boggs was out at the foul line stretching in preparation of his wind sprints, the operator stopped the clock—per Mauch's orders. The bewildered Boggs watched and waited as the clock remained stuck on 7:15. When five minutes had passed, the clock mysteriously jumped to 7:20, and Boggs had been flimflammed. Mauch said the story didn't have a happy ending for the Angels. "Since I never remember seeing Boggs go hitless against us, I figure he probably got his two or three hits anyway." Mauch never stopped the clock against Boggs again.

Joe DiMaggio

Joe DiMaggio was the epitome of class in uniform. He was the Fred Astaire of the diamond, Roy Hobbs in Yankee pinstripes. What would he need with a ritual when he had career statistics that placed him in the Hall of Fame on the first ballot and an aura that saw him named greatest living baseball player in 1975?

Perhaps it was his way of preparing to give his 100 percent on the field, but Joe D. had a pregame practice from which he never deviated . . . that is from which he only deviated once.

Arthur "Red" Patterson, an executive with the California Angels who has been connected with baseball for more than 60 years—as a newspaperman, PR director for the Yankees who originated the tape-measure home run and Old Timers' games, and executive with the Dodgers and Angels—tells this story about the Yankee Clipper and the 1951 World Series, his last appearance in Yankee pinstripes.

According to Patterson, it was no accident that DiMaggio became a spokesman for Mr. Coffee. Joe genuinely loved his coffee . . . still does.

As a player, DiMaggio was an inveterate coffee drinker. And before every game he would drink five or six cups of "joe" by his locker as he mentally prepared for the game. As a result he always came out to the field a little bit later than the rest of the team . . . always except that once.

In the 1951 Series, the defending champion New York Yankees (98–56 record) were expected to handle the NL champs, the New York Giants (98–59, beating the Brooklyn Dodgers in the Bobby Thomson "Giants win the pennant" play-off) in a classic crosstown rivalry.

The Yankees of Rizzuto, McDougald, DiMaggio, Berra, Bauer, Collins, Woodling, Brown, Mize, Lopat, Reynolds, Raschi, and a rookie named Mantle figured to feast on the Giants of Lockman, Dark, Irvin, Stanky, Thomson, Westrum, Koslo, Jansen, Maglie, and a rookie wonder named Mays.

But things were tougher than expected, and when Eddie Stanky, the feisty second baseman for the Giants, kicked the ball out of Yankee shortstop Phil Rizzuto's glove on a stolen base attempt in the fifth inning of game three at the Polo Grounds, the Giants erupted for five runs to take a 6–2 victory and a 2–1 lead over the Yankees.

Now, the Yankees felt that "Scooter" Rizzuto was made to look bad on what had been a very easy tag situation. It was embarrassing to the Yankees of that era to lose this way and to have a player like Stanky show up one of their most popular ballplayers.

Game four was set to begin at the Polo Grounds, and the Yankees were in the visitors' clubhouse, which was in center field, some 500 feet from home plate. Patterson recalls that usually players would saunter out to the field in groups of twos and threes. But this was different.

A couple of guys had begun to head onto the field, when

Yankee coach Frankie Crosetti called a team meeting—the Yankees never had team meetings in those days.

"Cro" said, "Wait a minute, you guys. Today, we're all going out like a team. We'll show those sons of bitches they can't [expletive] with the Yankees."

The team looked toward manager Casey Stengel for guidance. He winked and clapped his hands and said Crosetti was right.

As they started to hit the field en masse, they looked silently to DiMaggio, who had just started a ritual cup of coffee.

Without a word, Joe took a fast sip of his coffee and said, "You're damn right. We're Yankees. Let's show 'em what we're made of."

He got dressed, and the entire squad of 1951 New York Yankees ran out on the field together, creating a spine-tingling presence, to the roar of the crowd, and, led by DiMaggio (a single and a two-run homer), who had been hitless in the first three Series games, won game four, 6–2, en route to sweeping the final three games of the Series, to return the flag to Yankee Stadium.

DiMaggio closed out his career by belting out six hits in the final three games, with two doubles, a homer, and five RBIs.

Babe Ruth

If Joe DiMaggio looked like Fred Astaire in Yankee pinstripes, then Babe Ruth looked like Fred Flintstone. He hit a ton, weighed the same, and his ritual hygienic habits left much to be desired.

For Ruth, the game was the thing . . . that, and some food, drink, and a warm woman. Other things were of little import, so after a game, Ruth would shower, shave, and then put on the same underwear he had worn during the game, wearing the sweat-stained cotton under his expensive silk shirts and suits, day in and day out.

Teammates got on Babe (rightfully so) for that ritual, but Babe had the last word—he stopped wearing underwear altogether.

Luis Tiant

"Looey," who is worthy of a big book on oddities all by himself, was known for his long, dark, aromatic—read that "offensively billowing"—Cuban cigars. The Cuban-born right-hander, for the Cleveland Indians, Boston Red Sox, New York Yankees, and three other teams over a 19-year career, would often light his tobacco torches up. But on cue, his routine following a victory on the mound included a blazing postgame cigar, on which he would puff away while he was taking a shower. And never, according to teammates, did the waterfall extinguish his mouth torch, which was always still smoking away when Tiant finished his hygienic water blast.

He was also said to rub a mixture of marijuana and honey on his arm and elbow whenever tenderness overtook him. Tiant swore by the concoction, and his 229 wins and 49 shutouts over 19 years attest to its curative powers.

As to where he got the marijuana? Playful speculation was that he simply ground up some of those long Cuban cigars.

Rod Carew

"Sports Look"'s (ESPN) Roy Firestone likes to tell the story of Rod Carew, the celebrated Canal Zone native, who was meticulous about his bats. Carew carefully, methodically, put them in a soft place, kept them away from bad bats, weeded them out from their brother and sister bats of lesser wood, and kept them in a warm, caring environment.

According to Carew, "All good hitters take care of their bats. I made sure there was no pine tar buildup—even one ounce of dirt and tar makes the bat heavier—and would never bang them around or do anything to chip the wood."

Carew stored his bats in warm places—in a warm room in his house in the off-season—and kept them comfortable in a bed of sawdust to "help draw out any moisture."

The 19-year veteran second baseman—first baseman smacked out 3,053 hits by going with the pitch and using his wrists to slap the ball to safety. To get the right feel, he would also grind down his bats to make sure they were the proper width for him to wield.

Chico Salmon

Firestone also remembered that another Panamanian, Chico Salmon, would sleep with his bats. We don't know all the particulars of this sleeping arrangement, but the bats only responded to the tune of a .249 average. Was it something he said?

And Salmon, the utility infielder-outfielder for the Cleveland Indians and Baltimore Orioles over a nine-year career, kept a doll with removable parts in his locker. If his arm hurt, Salmon would remove the doll's arm and wear it around his neck, and soon his arm would feel better. If he had a headache, the doll's head would come off, and if his leg hurt, the doll leg would end up around Salmon's neck.

A believer in voodoo, Salmon also used an occasional doll or fetish to get the better of an opponent through the use of pins, water, or bat bashing.

Tony Gonzales

Tony Gonzales, a popular Cuban-born outfielder with the Philadelphia Phillies and four other teams from 1960 to 1971, kept a doll and would often dress it in the uniform of the opposing team. He'd then stick pins in it or bash it with his bat or step on it with his cleats, hoping that it would help his team win. Gonzales, who hit .286 in 1,559 games, also kept a small altar in his locker and would gladly help out teammates with a chant or two if they needed to kick a slump.

Tito Fuentes

Another devotee of voodoo was Tito Fuentes of the San Francisco Giants. Fuentes sprayed what he called "voodoo juice" on his glove, uniforms, body parts, and anything else he felt needed help.

A 13-year veteran who hit .268 in 1,499 games for the Giants and three other teams, Fuentes was also known to fill his baseball pants pockets with a voodoo combination pouch that included dusts, powders, beads, teeth, eagle's claw, turtle shells, and some things which are best left unspoken.

Other practicers of voodoo rights and rituals have included **Bobo Newsom,** the much-traveled hurler of the '20s, '30s, '40s, and '50s; **Urban Shocker,** the Yankees and Browns hurler who won 187 games in 13 years (four consecutive 20-win seasons); **Ross Grimsley,** the Montreal Expos odd 20-game winner in 1978, who had some bad times in Baltimore earlier in his career and once called in a renowned local voodoo woman to perform black magic and exorcise his poor luck (he had mixed results); and, some say, **Pascual Perez,** the outspoken hurler for the New York Yankees.

Bobby Bragan and Birdie Tebbetts

Concerning what loosely qualifies as a ritual of sorts, Bobby Bragan tells this story about himself. He followed Birdie Tebbetts as manager of the Milwaukee Braves in 1963. When Tebbetts vacated the premises, he left his replacement two envelopes, labeled "No. 1" and "No. 2," with the warning: "Open only in case of crisis."

Bragan had managed for about a year and a half—he went 84 and 78 in '63 but started slowly in '64—when the team began going poorly. The fans, the media, and the Braves front office were screaming for a change, so Bragan opened up the first envelope. Inside was a note which read: "Blame it on me and the old guys."

Bragan went to the front office and said, "You've saddled me with an old Adcock, Logan, Bruton, and Burdette. Birdie left me with a terrible team. I can't win with these old guys here. Get me younger players."

Pretty soon, the Braves stopped their slide, and Bragan's job was safe. Bragan's Braves went 88 and 74 in '64 and 86 and 76 in '65.

About two years later, the Braves were playing poorly and the fans were holding signs reading, "Bragan Must Go." The media and the brass clamored for Bragan's departure. Bragan dutifully went to his desk drawer and opened envelope number two. In it was a note that read, "Prepare two more envelopes."

Bragan was gone after 112 games of the '66 season, with a 52–59–1 mark.

Mort Cooper

Cecil Morton Cooper, brother of Walker Cooper and a right-handed pitcher who toiled in the National League from 1938 to 1949, winning 128 games (21 or more during three straight years from '42 to '44) with a 2.97 ERA, thought numbers were the key. Stalled on win number 13, in 1942 for the St. Louis Cardinals, he began changing his uniform number with every win, to match his win total, and after becoming number 21 (his last win), he won the league's MVP award.

Max Lanier

Max Lanier, a lefty control pitcher who won 108 games over a 14-year career spent mostly with the St. Louis Cardinals, took note from Cooper's success and would change his number whenever he won a game in 1943 or 1944. With each win, he would change uniforms and put on a new one with the next higher number. An interesting item to note is that 1943 and 1944 were by far his most productive seasons. Lanier went 15–7 in '43 and 17–12 in '44. He never won more than 13 before his uniform roulette, or more than 11 afterward. The act of revolving unis got to be too tough for the bookkeepers, so it was discontinued, otherwise Lanier might have worn numbers 20, 21, 22, and 23 before he retired in 1953.

Carlton Fisk

Future Hall-of-Fame catcher Carlton Fisk, of the Chicago White Sox, has been in the game for 20 years. Still agile at 42, "Pudge" takes ground balls in the infield before each game . . . except at Anaheim Stadium (California Angels) and Arlington Stadium (Texas Rangers). According to Fisk, "Those are the worst two infields in baseball."

Leo "The Lip" Durocher

Vin Scully, the Dodgers' play-by-play chief, remembers that, when Leo "The Lip" Durocher was third-base coach for Los Angeles, he would methodically erase the chalk lines from the third-base coach's box in which he was stationed. Usually by the end of the second inning, Leo had the lines etched out, but when he coached in artificial turf stadiums with painted-on lines, he nearly broke his feet trying to do the impossible . . . and it nearly drove him crazy.

Nolan Ryan

Soon to be Hall-of-Famer Nolan Ryan, of the Texas Rangers, rides a stationary bicycle after each start. About an hour after becoming the oldest man to throw a no-hitter (June 11, 1990), Ryan was seen riding to nowhere on his bike. He rides and rides and rides all the time—after his

5,000th strikeout, after his 299th win, after his first no-decision try at his 300th win—win, lose, or ND. His comment: "You don't deviate from routine." True to form, wins 300 and 301 were also followed by a Ryan "Tour declubhouse."

Tom Seaver

Ryan's ex-teammate, 311-game winner Tom "Tom Terrific" Seaver, exuded class on the mound during his 20-year career with the New York Mets, Cincinnati Reds, Chicago White Sox, and Boston Red Sox. His pregame routine involved doing crossword puzzles before games.

Seaver said, "The crossword puzzles relaxed me, but also got my mind exercised, as thinking how to get out of difficult spots—in the puzzles—relates to thinking on the mound and getting out of tough spots there."

Seaver also stayed away from interviews with the press before games, so as not to interfere with his concentration.

Steve Stone

Baltimore Orioles Cy Young winner Steve Stone (25–7 in 1980) was said to be "in a different world from the rest of us." But perhaps he was just ahead of his time and too "New Age" for his less-enlightened teammates.

Stone's pregame ritual included taking exactly the same route to the ballpark, stopping at the same restaurant and eating the same meal (see chapter 5), then stopping at another restaurant for another meal before he'd arrive at the park.

Once there—and this is what unnerved his teammates—he would sit alone in the dark for an hour and practice transcendental meditation and mind visualization techniques.

Stone would listen to a softly playing rock-and-roll tape on his cassette player and would visualize success. He said, "I associated it all with a winning pattern . . . a link to success. It was a mentalism or mindset to get the most out of myself."

Mike Cuellar

Perhaps the most consistent pitcher in baseball from 1969 through 1974 (125 wins and four 20-win seasons in six years) was Baltimore's Mike Cuellar. Cuellar was also one of the most superstitious players to ever play the game.

Among his pregame rituals was to wear blue—not just something borrowed, something blue, but all blue, head-to-toe blue. On days he was scheduled to start, Cuellar would always arrive at the park in his blue automobile and come in wearing blue shoes, blue socks, blue pants, blue belt, blue shirt, blue tie . . . and, sometimes, a blue jacket as well.

And from 1969 to 1976, Cuellar always wore the same baseball cap. During one start in Cleveland in 1975, on the first game of a road trip, Cuellar realized he had left his lucky Orioles cap in Baltimore. He flatly refused to pitch without it, so the Orioles had to send a plane for the cap. Orioles executives saw to it that the hat was put on a plane, so that it arrived in Cleveland and was ushered to the ballpark just moments before Cuellar was to take the mound.

Buoyed by the arrival of his chapeau, Cuellar proceeded to shut out the Indians for a Baltimore victory.

On another occasion, Cuellar was not so lucky. He left his cap behind as the team set down in Milwaukee. The procedure was known, and after a change of planes and a hand delivery, the hat arrived in time for Cuellar to take the hill, This time, however, Cuellar was given the hat, and as he started for the field, he shouted, "They sent the wrong cap. This isn't my game cap. This is my practice cap."

Cuellar got stomped, as the Brewers tagged him early and often. He stormed off the field in the third inning, threw down the impostor cap, and stomped on it to let it know how he felt.

"Wahoo Sam" Crawford

For no apparent reason, Samuel "Wahoo Sam" Crawford, the Hall-of-Fame outfielder (19 years from 1899 to 1917 with the Cincinnati Reds and Detroit Tigers, .309 avg.) and career leader in triples (312), would yell like hell whenever he ran around the bases. His nickname actually came not from his yelping around the bags but from the fact that he was born in Wahoo, Nebraska. Whatever the reason, his yelling usually startled opponents, who were not used to such abuse, into errors and missed tags, hence his high number of triples, doubles (457), and stolen bases (366).

"Ubbo Ubbo" Hornung

According to SABR's supreme nickname researcher, Jim Skipper, another guy who yelled like a banshee was Boston Red Caps outfielder Michael Joseph "Ubbo Ubbo" Hornung. Hornung got his nickname by grunting "ubbo ubbo" at the top of his lungs whenever he ran around the bases during his 12-year career for Boston and three other clubs from 1879 to 1890. The guttural chant paid off with 41 steals in 1887 and 1,230 hits in 1,123 games.

Roy White

Roy White, the classy outfielder for the New York Yankees from 1965 to 1979, ended his career in Japan, playing for the Yomiuri (Tokyo) Giants (1980 to 1982). While there, White received a roomful of Japanese talismans, tokens, and good luck charms, many of which came from Buddhist temples. Though not a Buddhist himself, White took the offerings to heart. He said, "It didn't hurt to rub them," so he rubbed them before every game and, in 1980, hit a career-high 29 homers for the Tokyo club, having never hit more than 22 for the Yanks.

Willie Davis

Another American, or *gaijin* as they are called in the Japan Leagues, who found peace in the East was ex-Dodger Willie Davis, an 18-year veteran of 2,429 games with six teams.

Davis was a deeply religious man who was a member of the Nichiren Buddhist religion. Signing with the Chunichi Dragons, Davis thought he'd be surrounded with players who would be responsive to his spiritual needs.

He was, however, more deeply religious than his teammates, to the point of antagonism. Davis ritualistically pulled out his beads and chanted monotonously before each game. Fellow players said Davis's chanting disrupted their *wa* or team unity.

Despite putting up good numbers in Japan—.306 and 25 homers before injuring his wrist—Davis was traded upon season's end, much to the good *wa* of the Dragons.

More ritual clips and bits and those who practiced them:

Marty Marion, the flashy shortstop for the St. Louis Cardinals and St. Louis Browns from 1940 to 1953, was known as "The Octopus" for his ability to grab anything in sight as a fielder. He was also a one-man ground crew. He picked up real and imaginary pebbles wherever he went, most notably while grooming the ground around his area at short and the territory near where he hit at home plate. He said the procedure was used to limber up his back, but others think he wanted a clean fielding area and some good luck stones.

Chicago Cubs shortstop **Shawon Dunston,** a slick-fielding, accurate-throwing, fielding wizard, lines up first base before every pitch with an imaginary throw from his shortstop position. He hasn't overthrown the bag once . . . on these visualization tosses.

Hall-of-Fame manager **Bucky Harris,** the skipper of the pennant-winning 1924 Washington Senators (he went on to manage for 29 years for eight teams) thought a certain young fan, 11-year-old Bradley Wilson, was a good luck charm, so he made sure he was in the stands for all home games by getting him to the ballpark in a chauffeured limousine.

Luke Sewell, manager of the St. Louis Browns from 1941 to 1948 (he later managed the Cincinnati Reds), kept all of his team's gloves with him over night and on off-days for luck. The plan worked in 1944, a pennant-winning year for the Brownies, but failed him the rest of the time, with no other finish higher than third.

"Smiling Stan" Hack, Chicago Cubs manager from 1954 to 1956, always spent the first inning of every game coaching third base for luck before he went into the dugout to manage. His ritual got him fired after finishes of seventh, sixth, and eighth during his three-year tenure.

Tommy Lasorda, the newly svelte manager of the Los Angeles Dodgers (he's been at their helm since 1976 and has six NL West flags to show for his time there), emulates Hack whenever the Dodgers go slumping. If the "Big Blue Wrecking Crew" loses a few games in a row, expect Lasorda to take a position out in the third-base coach's box to change his and the team's luck. As soon as the Dodgers win a game or two, not wanting to use up his lucky maneuver, Lasorda returns to his customary position in the dugout.

Former Los Angeles Dodgers executive and a fill-in second baseman for the 1943 Brooklyn Dodgers, **Al Campanis** goes back to his Greek heritage by collecting Greek pins and charms. He often hides them in home-baked pita bread and serves them to guests. To find any of the treasures is worth certain good luck, and Campanis, who found good fortune when he found such hidden gifts, discovered the trinkets before the 1963 and 1965 seasons, and both years he was rewarded with Dodger pennants.

Dave Winfield, the six-foot-six slugger who spent nine strong years with the New York Yankees (five consecutive 100 RBI seasons, a .340 average in 1984 and .322 in 1988) following a spectacular career start with the San Diego Padres (averaging 22 homers per year, 118 RBIs in 1979), has taken his ritual back out west to his new home, the California Angels. Winnie wears a great deal of jewelry on his wrists—watch, chains, and so on—and instead of taking it off to play, he tapes it over with white adhesive tape. That way he doesn't lose anything, can keep an eye on the jewelry (lockers have been broken into in the past), and still has the luck of keeping it with him.

For many years in New York, Winfield wore a *mazuzeh,* a religious object revered by members of the Jewish faith. Though Winfield is not Jewish, he had been befriended by and welcomed into a family that practiced Judaism. They honored him with the religious object, and Winfield responded by wearing it on and off the field as a matter of respect and ritual.

Sherman Lollar, catcher for the White Sox, Browns, Yankees, and Indians over an 18-year career, ritualistically stuffed his locker with four-leaf clovers for luck. It served him to the extent that he played in 1,752 games, belted 155 home runs, saw action in two World Series, and in 14 of his 18 seasons committed five errors or less.

Maybe if I drink more coffee, run laps on schedule, go to a Greek restaurant, scream like a banshee when I run the bases, prepare two envelopes, and find a lucky cap, there's still time for an exciting and rewarding career in professional baseball.

3
Batters

Second only to pitchers in mannerisms, twitches, routines, dances, prances, and superstitions, batters use these rituals as a means of defying bad luck, beating the pitcher at his own game, and mentally preparing to succeed at the toughest assignment in sports—hitting a curving, dipping, rising, knuckling, or speeding round ball with a moving round bat, an accomplishment of which it has been said a 30-percent success rate will make you a Hall-of-Famer . . . or at least a multimillionaire.

Don Mattingly, the classy and classic New York Yankee first baseman with the sweet swing and dedicated work ethic, says, "I don't have any superstitions or rituals," but check him out in the on-deck circle (or near it) before every at bat. He will not stay in the on-deck circle—never. He will creep up closer to home plate—an illegal area, actually—and take practice swings against the pitcher, who's throwing to the preceding batter. Mattingly says he sees the pitcher better from there and gets his timing down better (first half of 1990 notwithstanding), and his .323 career batting average indicates that his is an effective ritual.

Rituals? Superstitions? Nervous tics? Religious homage? Muscular-electric twinges? You be the judge. Anyway, they're fun to watch and most of the hitters who employ—or who can't stop—these gyrations are successful stars who'd make your rotisserie lineup anytime, twitches or not.

Next time you're at a ballgame, watch the hitters.

They're not jittery; they're purposeful. Have fun—jot down their motions and send them to me. I'll give you credit in my next book.

Crosses

Religion plays an important part in the game, but the old adage is "Praying only helps a batter if he can hit."

Luis Aparicio, the shortstop who made the Hall of Fame with his glove and speed (506 stolen bases) rather than with his bat and hit a solid .262 over an 18-year career spent mostly with the White Sox and Orioles, paid respect to his God by carefully crossing himself before each at bat. Most pitchers respected Aparicio's religious commitment, but one in particular didn't.

Early Wynn, the Hall-of-Fame hurler who won 300 games during a 23-year career with the Washington Senators, Cleveland Indians, and Chicago White Sox, was a fastball pitcher who gained a deserved reputation for being mean. It was said of Wynn, "He'd knock down his own mother if she stood in against him." Wynn seemed to delight in intimidating—and dusting off, brushing back, and nailing—opposing hitters.

When he saw Aparicio crossing himself at the plate, Wynn, from sixty-feet-six-inches away, yelled, "Don't go crossing yourself when you face me."

Aparicio ignored him and continued his religious ritual.

Wynn again yelled for "Little Looey" to cease, apparently taking it as a personal affront.

Aparicio, now annoyed, recrossed himself, whereupon Wynn, heretofore not considered a religious man, crossed himself as well.

Aparicio saw this and asked the pitcher, "Wynn, you're not Catholic. Why are you crossing yourself?"

Wynn yelled back, "It's to show God that I'm going to knock you on your ass with the next pitch."

And he did, with a fastball aimed at Aparicio's head.

Jimmy Piersall, the enigmatic outfielder for the Boston Red Sox, Cleveland Indians, California Angels, and Washington Senators, hit a solid .272 over a 17-year career. He methodically drew two crosses, side by side, in the corner of the right batter's box before every at bat. His was an homage to his creator, and he was unerring in this ritual.

Piersall, for you trivia buffs, may have been the first batter to wear a helmet with ear flaps. After belting two home runs off Detroit pitcher **Pete Burnside** in 1960, Piersall clowned around and showed up the hurler. Former teammate **Rocky Colavito,** who was then with the Tigers, warned Piersall that he was going to be the bull's-eye in some Tiger pitching–shooting gallery practice, so Piersall grabbed a Little League helmet, complete with two ear flaps.

Piersall was almost thrown out by the umpire for wearing it to the plate, and Chicago Cub manager Lou Boudreau (who wasn't even involved in this) called him gutless. Piersall himself recalled that the wind whipped through the ear holes and he felt as if he were in a huge seashell, but he wore the helmet anyway. Twenty years later, virtually every ballplayer would wear ear-flapped helmets.

Rico Carty, a 15-year major leaguer who hit .299 and 204 homers for six teams (Braves, Indians, and others), would draw crosses in the batter's box for peace of mind and dedication to the task at hand. Former teammate catcher **Joe Torre** was traded to St. Louis in 1969, and when Carty, with Atlanta, would come to bat and draw his crosses, Torre would erase them. It got to be more than a joke, but Torre felt he'd gained the upper hand.

Torre, by the way, admitted that while at the plate as a hitter, he would take off his helmet to show his mother he had gotten a new haircut as she wanted. His haircuts may have taken their toll on his hair, but as an 18-year player with the Braves, Cardinals, and Mets, his .297 career average, one batting title (.363 in 1971), 252 home runs, and 1,185 RBIs (137 in 1971) indicate that his helmet doffing didn't affect a picture swing.

Cincinnati Reds shortstop **Davey Concepcion** drew a cross at the plate before each at bat for 19 years and has said, "If I hit .300 or .200 [his career mark was .267], the honor paid would be the same. It was God's will that made me a ballplayer."

Candy Maldonado, the fine young outfielder of the Cleveland Indians, draws the cross. "It's a part of me," he said. He walks in front of home plate, never behind it, and draws his sign. "It feels weird if I do it any other way," he said.

Many other players put crosses in the dirt, or cross themselves before each at bat, but most do it surreptitiously.

Deion Sanders

Two-sport athlete "Neon" Deion Sanders ("Yes, I'm a Yankee; yes, I'm an Atlanta Falcon") is a young star on the gridiron and a "wanna be" on the diamond, who has already endeared himself to bench jockeys (and Carlton Fisk) by failing to utilize his great speed to run out routine pop-ups and ground balls. Sanders goes religion one step further. He, too, scratches in the dirt as he steps into the batter's box. But instead of emulating Piersall and others by drawing religious crosses in the clay, Sanders answers to a higher authority, the "almighty dollar," as the young

outfielder uses his bat to dig a dollar sign in the batter's box before he faces the opposing hurler. So far, it has resulted in a lackluster career batting average, hovering around the "Mendoza Line," but the dollar sign modus operandi seems to have worked . . . at least financially. In July 1990, while batting an anemic .158, Sanders was offered a 1991 contract with the Yankees that would have paid him (if incentives were met) a whopping $2.5 million. This, after he had signed a $4.4 million contract with the NFL's Atlanta Falcons. The Yankees eventually pulled back the huge offer, but Sanders, considering his output, was still raking up an inordinate number of dollar signs.

Maybe dollar signs *do* make the difference.

[*Author's note:* The New York Yankees' Deion Sanders experiment marks the third time in recent years that the Yankees have gone hard after a football player. They signed John Elway (first round draft choice in 1981) to a Minor League contract, and he played well at first base before giving up the sport to excel on the gridiron; and they made Bo Jackson a first round draft choice out of high school in 1982 (he was listed as a shortstop), but he decided to go on to college and two-sport success. Sanders, an outfielder, was drafted in the thirtieth round of the 1988 draft.]

Joe Morgan

Indelibly etched in the mind's eye of baseball fans from 1963 to 1984, from Houston to Cincinnati, was solid but pint-sized left-handed hitting second baseman Joe Morgan's pump-pump-pump of his left arm and elbow, as he prepared to receive the pitcher's next offering. Morgan used it to set himself for each pitch—timing was part of it—and to remind himself to keep his left shoulder up in preparation for a line drive swing that produced 268 homers and two .300 seasons. He won two NL MVPs and a Hall of Fame election, so the pump worked for him.

Vic Power

Morgan's pump was similar to that of a predecessor, Vic Power, a golden-gloved, sweet-swinging first baseman who toiled for Kansas City, Cleveland, California–Los Angeles, and Philadelphia from 1954 to 1965. Power hit .284 over his career, with three .300 seasons. The righty hitter would prepare for each pitch by swinging his bat pendulum style with his right hand, making a forward arc toward the pitcher until the bat met his left hand. His left hand would then rock back toward the mound, stop, and send the hunk of wood on its way back across home plate and toward the foul area stands. This back-and-forth routine would terminate after four or five swings and result in a deep crouch (Rickey Henderson—style) by Power, who would endeavor to uncoil and knock the next pitch in the gap for one of his 290 career doubles. He nonchalantly performed this pendulum act before every pitch.

Power should have been the first black Yankee. It was documented that the Yankee brass disliked his "aggressive attitude"—he basically felt all people were created equal and saw no difference between those of different skin color, thus he treated all people alike and wanted to be treated as an equal himself—and waited for an athlete with a more moderate attitude, Elston Howard, to emerge as the talent they required for their first black in pinstripes. The Yanks soon traded him out of their organization and on to the A's, for whom he enjoyed a solid career.

Wade Boggs

As Boggs, arguably baseball's best hitter, emphatically approaches another title—baseball's most superstitious player (see chapters 5 and 6)—he deviates slightly from the norm at the plate. While many players inscribe crosses, dollar signs, or personal hieroglyphics in the dirt around or in the batter's box prior to doing battle with the pitcher, Boggs brings in a variation. Though not Jewish, he carefully takes his bat and draws the Hebrew *chai* symbol in the earth before every at bat. *Chai,* which means "life," has brought life to Boggs's bat for a decade.

Billy Williams

The Chicago Cubs' consistent and graceful hitter Billy Williams sharpened his batting eye, and his hand-mouth coordination, by throwing himself spitballs, or more to the point, by spitting at himself.

At least once every game, he would intentionally "hit the spit." Williams would stride to the plate, sniff deeply, "hock one off," and swing his bat, blasting aside the expectoration before it hit the ground. Observers never saw him miss the saliva, and his .290 average and 426 career home runs provide proof that he didn't miss much else, either. Wonder how he'd have done against Ed Walsh (see chapter 4).

Stan "The Man" Musial

Hall-of-Fame batter extraordinaire Stan "The Man" Musial, the St. Louis Cardinal outfielder–first baseman with the sweetest swing in sports (.331 average, seven batting titles, 475 homers, 1,951 RBIs in 22 years), wiggled his hips like a belly dancer to loosen up during each at bat. Musial claimed it helped his mental concentration, physical relaxation, and to replant in his mind his own batting edict: "Don't hit a flyball to center field."

Jackie Robinson

Jack Roosevelt Robinson is the man generally regarded as being the first black in baseball. It is arguable that he was actually the ninth black to play Major League baseball and the 61st or so to play organized baseball (Minor Leagues). According to information provided by Richard Topp of SABR, Robinson was preceded by Moses Fleetwood "Fleet" Walker and his brother, Welday Walker, who played for the Toledo Blue Stockings of the American Association in 1884; Vincent "Sandy" Nava (reputed to be black, Providence Grays in 1882 and Baltimore Orioles in 1885); Bill Higgins (reputed to be black, Boston Beaneaters in 1888); George Treadway (reputed to be black, Baltimore Orioles in 1893, Brooklyn in 1894–95, Louisville in 1896); Armando Marsans (a Cuban, Cincinnati Reds in 1911, played until 1918, Cardinals and Yankees); Tex McDonald, born Charles Crabtree (reputed to be black, Cincinnati Reds in 1912, played until 1915 with Braves and Federal League teams); Ramon Herrera (Boston Red Sox in 1925–26, reputed to be black, sneaked in as a "Latin" player). Additionally, New York Giant manager John McGraw tried to sneak in black second baseman Charles Grant as an Indian—he renamed him Chief Tuckahoma in 1905, but was found out before Grant could play a game.

But Robinson was the man who finally broke, for all time, the color barrier in the sport, in 1947 with the Brooklyn Dodgers.

He was a Hall-of-Fame infielder (predominantly a second baseman) who maintained a career of substance in demeanor, courage, and accomplishment—10 years with the Brooklyn Dodgers, .311 career average, 137 homers, 197 stolen bases—though he was not allowed to play Major League ball until he was 28 years old.

Robinson also had a few quirks at the plate. Once set in the batter's box, the right-handed hitter would slap his right thigh with his right hand. And it was well known that Robinson would never go up to bat unless he could cross directly between the catcher and the pitcher. He would step where he had to—in front of home plate if necessary—to get in the middle of the opposing battery, and if there was a mound conference before Robinson hit, he would wait until the catcher left and returned to his spot behind the plate before he would continue his stroll and step up to the dish.

Gil Hodges

Another Dodger, Robinson's first baseman teammate Gil Hodges, put in a solid 18 years in the National League, producing 370 home runs and 1,274 RBIs. The six-foot-one-and-a-half, 200-pounder would tap home plate three times and adjust his cap after each pitch. Al Conin, the California Angels' announcer, recalls that Hodges's routine included adjusting his sleeves, straightening his helmet, and making sure his cup (crotch) felt right. He would also take his huge hands, and push his helmet back and spread his eyes apart so he could "see the ball better." This ritual took all of about five or six seconds, but he did it in each of nearly 8,000 at bats over 19 years.

And Hodges, being a family man, also blew a kiss to his wife each time he homered at Ebbets Field in Brooklyn.

Mike Hargrove

Mike Hargrove was called "The Human Rain Delay."

In a set routine that drove umpires, broadcasters, opposing pitchers, and even his own teammates crazy, Hargrove took time between every single pitch to fidget, scratch, adjust things, meditate, and stretch. He took time and took his time while he took time.

In 1,666 games over 12 years, Hargrove served as dh and played first base and the outfield for the Texas Rangers, San Diego Padres, and Cleveland Indians. During that time, in more than 6,500 at bats (including walks, sacrifice flies, and hit batsmen), figuring an average of five pitches per at bat, Hargrove must have wasted some 975,000 seconds, or 16,250 minutes, or 271 hours, with his routine. That means he spent more than eleven days at the plate just adjusting things.

A typical Hargrove war dance, repeated on each pitch, was to step out of the batter's box and meditate for a moment, take a batter's stance (still outside the box), take three swings with the bat before he entered the batter's box, adjust his right batting glove to make sure there were no creases in it, then adjust his left glove, then pull up his pants, put one foot in the batter's box, knock the dirt out of his cleats, tap the box with his bat, adjust his right sleeve, adjust his left sleeve, and refit his helmet . . . slowly . . . in that exact order.

Of the routine, Hargrove said, "I just did what I had to do to get ready. It was my key to total concentration. Even the recesses of my mind were thinking about each pitch as I went through my motions. I meditated on my stance, my swing, my visualization of the pitch, what and where the pitcher would throw. And if this unnerved the pitcher, so much the better. It gave me an edge."

"It didn't seem like a long time to me," he added.

The plan worked to the extent that Hargrove finished with five .300 seasons and a career mark of .290.

He summed up his habit this way: "The only difference at the Major League level, between a regular player and a star, is mental preparation."

Yet Hargrove says that Baltimore Orioles star Eddie Murray was consistently timed as taking longer at the plate than Hargrove. Murray moves dirt around the batter's box to the point of distraction. And Mike Terry, the San Bernardino Sun beat writer who regularly covers the American League, reports that Carlton Fisk usually takes longer than either one of them with the Fiskian routine.

Carlton Fisk

One of the classiest athletes to play the game over the last two decades is Carlton Fisk, the Hall-bound catcher for the Chicago White Sox. The Fisk home plate routine includes the following procedure: he steps into the batter's box with his right foot, grips the bat, loosens the grip and regrips it, pulls his shirt sleeves—first right, then left—

steps out, steps in again, gets his left foot ready, then takes three practice swings before he'll let the pitcher throw. It has worked for a .271 average and more than 350 home runs, covering nearly 2,300 games in 21 years.

Ted Williams

Ted Williams, "The Thumper," "The Splendid Splinter," perhaps the greatest pure hitter of the last 50 years, had his own home plate ritual, besides beating the heck out of opposing pitchers during his 19 years with the Boston Red Sox (six batting titles, the last .400 season—.406 in 1941— and a lifetime average of .344, with 521 homers and 1,839 RBIs despite losing seven peak seasons to service hitches). Teddy Ballgame's regular ritual involved tucking his bat under his right armpit and reaching up to tug hard on his cap and helmet. He only did this with two strikes on him.

Rod Carew

Rod Carew, the perennial batting leader for the Twins and the Angels, usually led off, and by the time his first at bat was finished, there would be no back line to the left-side batter's box. Carew would carefully erase that line with a few deft kicks and scrapes from his shoes. This, he reasoned, would allow him to stand a few inches—or even a foot—farther back from the pitcher than the rules allow, thereby giving him a blink more time to look over a pitch or begin his swing. It worked to the tune of seven batting crowns.

Eddie Collins

Hall-of-Fame second baseman Eddie Collins buried his bats in a compost pile. And if that wasn't enough for the 25-year veteran for the Philadelphia A's and Chicago White Sox, the omnipresent glob of gum on his cap was.

A career .333 hitter with 3,311 base hits in 2,826 games, "Cocky," as he was called, would stick a hunk of chewed gum on the button of his cap as he went to bat.

If the count went to two strikes, Collins would remove the gum, pop it into his mouth, and chew the sucker until he got a hit.

During one game in 1925, ChiSox teammate Ted Lyons sprinkled cayenne pepper on the rubbery chew, and when Collins went to an 0–2 count, he flipped the gum into his mouth, choked, spit, and let out a yell that was heard throughout Comisky Park.

He struck out on the next pitch but was not cured of his habit.

Ken Singleton

Ken Singleton, the sharp, switch-hitting, six-foot-four, 210-pound outfielder for the Baltimore Orioles and Montreal Expos, who spent 15 years in the Bigs, hitting a tough .282 with 246 homers, would pick up three pebbles before every appearance at bat. He'd toss them over his shoulder and dig in at the plate. Singleton said, "I did it to remind me that I have three strikes and that I should be selective. It helped me concentrate."

Harry "The Hat" Walker

Harry "The Hat" Walker, an 11-year Major League outfielder who played mostly for the Cardinals and Phillies, while batting .296 (he won the 1947 batting crown, posting a .363 mark) also earned his nickname by employing the following routine at the plate. He pulled his hat on and off three times, rubbed his forearm, and slicked his hair back before every pitch.

Babe Ruth

Babe Ruth spent hours "boning" his bat with a bone or bottle, to make the grain hard and the bat smooth. And this was after he went down to the Hillerich & Bradsby bat factory in Louisville, Kentucky, to personally pick out all his bats. Ruth used a 42-ounce monster at the plate, whereas today's players usually opt for something around 33 to 35 ounces. Ruth once used a 50-ounce club in practice, and it is said that Edd Roush, of the Giants and Reds, regularly pulled around a 48-ouncer.

Another Ruthism was never to lend any of his bats to a teammate. He explained, "Bats only have so many hits in them, and I deserve all the hits my bats can muster."

Up at the plate, the "Sultan of Swat" knocked the dirt (or imaginary dirt) out of his spikes with his bat after each strike. Balls apparently didn't get Babe dirty.

Cap Anson

Adrian Constantine "Cap" Anson was a great-hitting third baseman (.329, 3,000 hits, and 1,715 RBIs over 22 years) for the Chicago White Stockings and Chicago Colts from 1876 to 1897.

He may have been the first player to coddle his bats. He oiled them, dusted them, kept them warm, and massaged the pieces of wood before every game and during the off-season. He kept between one hundred and five hundred bats at his home during off-seasons when he took care of the entire team's supply, serving as player-manager from 1879 to 1897. His motto: "Be good to them and they'll be good to you." Even for 10 years following his retirement from the game, Anson oiled and dusted each of the 400 bats he kept in his basement.

On the downside, historically, Anson's motto didn't pertain to his fellow man. It was Anson, leader of the 1883 White Stockings of the National Association, who threatened to pull his all-white team off the field if Toledo Blue Stockings catcher Moses Fleetwood "Fleet" Walker, the first black to play Major League ball, played. Anson lost the bluff and the game went on.

Anson's bigoted stance soon gained steam, though, and by 1887, when Anson successfully got Walker and his black batterymate, pitcher George Stovey, removed from the Newark Little Giants (semi-pro) lineup in an exhibition game, the color barrier had been erected—not to fall for good for 70 years, when Jackie Robinson was picked up by the Brooklyn Dodgers.

Other twitching, wiggling batsmen who made their marks in baseball history include:

Chicago Cubs Hall-of-Famer **Ernie Banks,** who wiggled his fingers before each pitch and smacked 512 homers and 2,583 hits following the wiggles.

Hall-of-Fame second baseman **Frankie Frisch,** who hit .316 over 19 years for the Giants and Cardinals, from 1919 to 1937, scratched his right shoe up on his left stocking at each plate appearance. Frisch couldn't curb the habit and proceeded to employ the grasshopper maneuver while coaching at first base or third base later in his career.

Current players routinely mock multimillionaire slugger **Jose Canseco** and his neck twitch (a shrug to each shoulder—head goes to the side, shoulder comes up to meet the head) and occasional 360-degree bank before setting his massive six-foot-three, 200-pound frame toward belting the next pitch.

Jesus Alou, one of the hitting, outfielding Alou brothers (15-year career, .280 average) wielded his bat in helicopterlike fashion, whirling away before he got ready to hit.

Tito Fuentes did more with the bat after missing a pitch than he did when he connected. The second baseman from Cuba played nine years of a 13-year career with the San Francisco Giants and managed only a .268 average, though he did bat

.309 for Detroit in 1977. After a miss, Fuentes would routinely send the bat on a journey through his legs, behind his back, around his head, and in some places that defy explanation.

Mickey Rivers, the fleet-footed center fielder for the Angels, Yankees, Rangers, and others, would twirl his bat as a cheerleader uses a baton, after every swing-and-miss, switching the bat one-handed from one palm to the other. The technique was worth a .295 career mark through 15 seasons.

Willie Montañez spun his bat as though it were a baton whether he swung or took a pitch. The habit brought him a .275 average and three .300 seasons in 14 years with nine teams.

Cincinnati Reds star outfielder **Eric Davis** emulates Jackie Robinson and slaps his right thigh before each at bat.

Young California Angels outfielder **Dante Bichette** will stretch his back, sweep back and forth with his bat, dig in with his back foot, and stretch and touch his batting gloves prior to each pitch.

His teammate, first baseman **Wally Joyner,** taps each foot with his bat.

William "Swish" Nicholson, an outfielder for the Cubs and Phillies for 16 years, from 1936 to 1953, smacking 235 homers in the process, earned his nickname as he swished his bat through the air as though he were swatting flies, leading an orchestra, or sword fighting.

Rocky Colavito, power-hitting outfielder for the Cleveland Indians and Detroit Tigers, would always snap the bat across his back and shoulders before hitting. It loosened him up and allowed him to catch his breath and concentrate on the next pitch. Colavito lasted 14 years, won a home run title, and blasted 374 homers with 1,159 RBIs to go along with a .266 average.

Billy Herman, second baseman for the Chicago Cubs, routinely changed his stance several times during each game—often, several times during each at bat, depending on how he was going that day. Herman played 15 years, moving on to Chicago, Brooklyn, and Boston of the National League. His ever-changing stance brought him a .304 career average and a Hall-of-Fame election.

Philadelphia Phillies infielder **Tony Taylor** (.261 over 19 years) and Tiger-Dodger **Kirk Gibson** (hero of the 1988 World Series) like to work fast. They are no-nonsense men at the plate and want to hit. No delays, no changes, they just get up there and take their cuts.

Jeffrey Leonard, the "Hac-Man" for the Seattle Mariners, once made the quickest work of all. Playing for AAA Phoenix in 1981, Leonard announced that he would swing at the first pitch in every at bat for his entire stay there. He responded with a .401 average in 47 games, covering more than 200 trips to the plate. He was soon called up to the Giants, and he backed off . . . a little bit. He will now take the first pitch "when it feels right" for him to do so.

While the following are not visible mannerisms at the plate, these players loved and coddled their bats to such a degree that their inclusion seems a rational one.

Ted Williams, like Babe Ruth, made a yearly pilgrimmage to Louisville to find his personal "sluggers."

Italian **Joe DiMaggio** rubbed olive oil into his bats to keep the wood supple and resistant to breaking. He spent hours "boning" his war clubs and also sandpapered the handles to take one-half to three-quarters of an ounce of weight off the stick and give him a quicker swing.

Shoeless Joe Jackson took his bat, "Black Betsy," to bed with him for a warm cuddle.

Another love story of a boy and his bat involved **Kevin Elster** of the New York Mets. In 1988, Elster, the Mets infielder, took his bat to bed with him (details of the night are sketchy), and the next day, he belted a home run. Seizing the new relationship, Elster invited his bat to lunch the next day, and it responded by helping Elster bang out another four-bagger the following game. There's no word on how the relationship is going this year.

George Sisler hammered Victrola needles into his bats, then "boned" them in with a ham bone.

Honus Wagner boiled his bats in a creosote mixture.

Nellie Fox would bash his bats with a sledgehammer to smooth down the hitting surface.

Bobby Bonds spent hours sandpapering one side of his bat, smoothing it down for better contact.

Ted Kluzewski hammered nails into his bat to make it harder.

Mickey Mantle, Roger Maris, Bill "Moose" Skowron, and **Tony Kubek** carved the grain out of their bats, then replaced the missing wood with pine tar. They let it harden, then sanded it down to give their bats a harder hitting surface.

Many old stars and journeymen alike hammered nails, tacks, and screws into their bats and shaved one side to flatten the area. Most of the above was legal during the dawn of baseball, before the turn of the century.

Ex-Cubs slugger **Leon Durham** would have his mother pray over his bats before each season, but as they say, praying only helps if you're a good hitter.

It goes to show . . . different strokes for different folks. Whatever gets you through the night game. And if it works once, these guys are sure it will work over the long haul, day in and day out for 10 to 20 years . . . and just because a bad-hop single drove in a run for them in Little League. But then again, Hank Greenberg's comment "My only superstition is that I have to touch all four bases after hitting a home run" shows "it's all in the mind, you know."

I wonder if I can get the guys on my rotisserie team to pray, gyrate, chew gum, step out of the box, knock the dirt out of their spikes, and sleep with their bats. Maybe if I soak my lineup in creosote . . .

4
Pitchers

Why do pitchers get their own chapter? Because pitchers are the most superstitious, most ritualistic, most odd, and most idiosyncratic athletes on the diamond, without a doubt. Or maybe they just occupy the toughest position in sports and need these little edges as a means of preparation for that greatest of all one-on-one encounters (World Cup penalty kicks, hockey penalty shots, and the finals at Wimbledon notwithstanding), that of pitcher versus batter—instant success or failure some 27 to 40 times per game.

Do you want to have fun next time you're at a ballgame? Keep your eyes on the pitcher during warm-up throws and before each pitch. Chances are he'll be doing something irregular. But the twitches, jerks, touching of cap, chest, pocket, and face are not by mistake. They may be subconscious maneuvers, or rhythmic animated meditation techniques, but they are all part of his pre-pitch routine, and part of his mechanics.

Mike Cuellar

Some baseball superstition aficionados believe that a chapter on pitchers must begin and end with Mike Cuellar, the 15-year veteran, 185-game winner who spent most of his career with the Baltimore Orioles (four 20-win seasons).

Cuellar would place his glove at a certain spot near the end of the dugout after each Orioles inning in the field, drink some water, then light up a cigarette, which he would smoke until the first Oriole was retired. Then he'd Bogart that smoke, pick up his glove, and return to a special spot on the bench, forcing anyone else in that spot to vacate.

Following the last Oriole out, Cuellar would sit in the dugout until his catcher had begun putting on his second shin guard.

Once on the hill, Cuellar would not allow an opponent to throw him the baseball—he'd only accept it from a fellow Oriole. If a third-base coach threw it to him, he'd duck out of the way and wait for it to stop rolling, then pick it up.

Taking warm-ups before every inning, he had to pick the ball up from the ground and wouldn't allow anyone, Oriole or otherwise, to throw him the pill. Cuellar preferred to pick the ball up from the dirt, circle the mound, and walk up the second-base side of the hill before going into his warm-ups.

Don Bessent

While Babe Ruth *never did* stick his tongue out to telegraph his upcoming curveball, as William Bendix did portraying him in perhaps the worst and least accurate of all historical baseball movies, *The Babe Ruth Story,* former Brooklyn Dodgers hurler Don Bessent, a promising young hurler who bobbed in and out of the baseball scene from 1955 to 1958, did, in fact, show the old taste organ each time he threw the bender.

Bessent, with a blazing fastball and an adequate curve, was thought to have a chance at being a 20-game winner when the Dodgers first brought him up, but he was moved to the bull pen when it was thought by manager Walt Alston that his heater could best be utilized in an inning or two in relief, along with firemen Clem Labine and Ed Roebuck.

It was during a relief stint in the Fall Classic that Bessent's telegraphing tongue was first read. The Dodgers met the Yankees in the 1956 World Series, and in the final game, the Bronx Bombers had touched Brooklyn starter Don Newcomb for four runs in three innings. With the Dodgers down 4–0, Bessent came in to hurl the fourth. He was hammered. Every time Bessent prepared to bend off a curve, the Yankee dugout would let fly with a chorus of whistles. The Dodgers couldn't figure out why the Yanks were serenading them, or why their pitcher was getting hit so hard.

Later, word filtered over to Bessent that he was tipping off his pitch with an errant tongue. He kept his tongue in his mouth, but lost his rhythm, hurt his arm, and was soon out of The Show.

Bessent, who compiled a 14–7 won-lost mark and a 3.33 ERA in 108 games for the Dodgers, with a 1–0, 1.35 ERA in five World Series appearances in '55 and '56, developed arm trouble and was shipped to the minors in 1959. He retired in 1962 after four seasons in the Bushes.

Johnny Podres

One of Bessent's pitching buddies with the Brooks was lefty hurler Johnny Podres. For 15 years with the Dodgers, Tigers, and Padres, Podres was Mr. Consistency, compiling 12 or more wins, 31 or more games pitched, and 182 or more innings pitched, for seven straight years, on his way to 148 career wins and appearances in four World Series. Johnny was known as a "night person," and some of his roommates admitted to seeing more of Johnny's luggage than they did of Johnny. Johnny's nighttime ritual usually involved wine, women, and song—he said it gave him better nerves on the mound, but one part of Podres's pitching ritual was to abstain from sex the night before he was to pitch. He swore by that rule. When one team official questioned Podres on the practice, the left-hander was serious when he said, "No. I do not have sex the night before a game. Two or three nights before, sure. That's OK, but not the night before."

Randy Johnson

On June 2, 1990, Seattle Mariner ace Randy Johnson made baseball history when, at six feet ten, he became the tallest pitcher ever to fire a Major League no-hitter, by blanking the Detroit Tigers. And Johnson had help—musical help.

During the '89–'90 off-season, Randy was given something he had wanted since childhood: a set of drums. He began banging out riffs on the skins and found that it relaxed him. He took to playing the instrument whenever things got tense around the house or following a rough game on the mound.

On the afternoon of June 2, the tall left-hander played his drums for an hour and a half, finishing up just before he left for the ballpark.

Then came the no-hit bid. Through seven innings, he hadn't given the possibility of such a success much thought, but by the eighth frame, knowing he'd have to face Lou Whitaker, Allen Trammell, and Cecil Fielder again before getting the first no-hitter in Seattle history, his nerves began to percolate to the surface.

Attempting to regain his composure, Johnson began imagery—playing his drums in his mind, visualizing the rim shots and the drum rolls and the rhythm of the beat. He began to tap his hand on his knee and to relax. Musically content, Johnson mowed down the Bengals in the eighth and ninth to record the no-no, and now, often, you'll see him twitching or tapping on the bench or on the mound. That's not twitching, it's just the drum solo from "In-a-Gadda-da-Vida."

Mark "The Bird" Fidrych

One of the great supernovas in baseball history was Mark "the Bird" Fidrych, the Rookie-of-the-Year pitcher for the Detroit Tigers in 1976 (19—9 with a 2.34 ERA).

Fidrych was thought to talk to the ball, the mound, and opposing bats, but in reality, he was preparing himself for the task at hand—getting opposing hitters out—which he did with startling efficiency during his rookie year.

Typical Fidrych behavior was to get down on his hands and knees and manicure the pitcher's mound. He'd remove paper, pebbles, and ruts, and make certain he had a smooth surface. But seeing a glamorous baseball player rolling around the ground seemed a bit strange.

Once on the mound, he actually appeared to be talking to the baseball. He'd urge that pellet to help him get the next hitter, and he'd make friends with the sphere. What he was actually doing was meditating and visualizing the next out, enhancing his confidence level while getting a mental jump on the annoyed hitter.

Following a hit, Fidrych would become unhappy with the ball he had just taken into his confidence, and he'd throw the offending pill out of the game. Once he told an umpire, "No, thank you. I don't want this ball . . . it has a hit in it." He urged the ump to take the ball back and put it in the bag with the other balls, who could convince this bad ball to pop up the next hitter as a good ball should.

Resembling the gawky Big Bird character for which he was nicknamed, Fidrych would also run around the infield and outfield and congratulate his fielders on great plays . . . a nice thing to do, but generally unheard of in staid Major League circles.

Bert Blyleven

Bert has put up some very Hall-of-Fame-like numbers during a career that has spanned 21 years and six teams—currently California. He is bearing down on 300 wins, is getting close to 3,750 strikeouts, and is already eighth on the all-time shutout list. His pranks, which are legendary, are designed to get a team going good. A favorite of his is setting fire to the shoelaces of ballplayers and writers, who are then unaware that their feet are ablaze.

He also has a warm-up routine. He will start every inning's warm-up tosses with—in this exact order—four fastballs, two curves, and one change-up, then work on what is necessary.

Blyleven will also sit in exactly the same place in the dugout whenever he pitches, and will kick and erase foul lines and coaching lines. He lamented, "On artificial turf, the lines are painted in and I can't erase them. Someday I'll figure out how and . . ."

Charlie Hough

According to *Orange County Register* columnist Susan Gaede, "Good Time" Charlie, the veteran Texas Ranger knuckleballer, is the consummate Elvis Presley fan and nearly always wears one of his assortment of Elvis Presley commemorative T-shirts under his uniform. He denies it and refuses to pose in his T-shirt, but there are rumors that he hums "Hound Dog" or "Jailhouse Rock" before letting fly with a clutch knuckleball.

Rob Murphy

Murphy, the Boston Red Sox fireman (273 relief appearances in the approximately three-and-a-half years from 1987 to 1989), makes this book on at least two counts, and both involve appearance. One May, 1990, evening at the Kingdome in Seattle, saw Murphy take the mound in the eighth, with the job of protecting a three-run BoSox lead. He saw that lead evaporate to one, after he gave up two runs on two hits and three walks in the eighth. After the last out, he stormed into the Boston clubhouse, picked up a razor, and shaved his four-day beard.

Armed, or faced, with a new look, he blazed down the side in the Seattle ninth and preserved the Red Sox victory.

Murphy's other entry into the superstitious comes from the fireballer's ritual of wearing black bikini underwear beneath his baseball pants every game.

Yes, that 95-mph fastball is being thrown by a guy in black bikini underwear.

According to Murphy, his career was at a low ebb, while playing A ball at Cedar Rapids in 1983, when this fastball wizard began throwing a knuckleball as a last resort to keep himself in baseball. He was turned into a reliever and tried to learn the slider but was getting hit hard each time he took the mound.

To loosen him up, Murphy's grandmother sent him a batch of "funky, kinky" underwear, and as a joke, the pitcher wore some black briefs, and pitched well—his first good outing in weeks. He continued to wear the bikinis and pitched 18 innings while allowing only one run to end the season.

The next year he was promoted to AA ball at Vermont and, forgetting his good luck panties, gave up 11 runs in nine innings of work.

While going over his mechanics, he sorted through his duffel bag and found the pair of black undies he had worn the year before, realized he had forgotten about them and hadn't worn them since last season, washed them, put them on, and went out and pitched three perfect innings of relief, striking out eight. His next outing, he went three innings of perfect ball and struck out 6 and a superstition was born.

Murphy has worn the black bikinis ever since (he has several pairs now but wears them in every game).

And it is noteworthy that he dresses and undresses certain body parts in the exact same order every game.

Another Murphy ritual occurs on the mound. He lines up the resin bag in the middle of the field, on a direct line between second base and home plate, and steps on the rubber deliberately, using the same motion every time.

Murphy also deserves special recognition as a colorful ritualist. Following a shellacking he had taken on the mound one night at Fenway, Murphy threw his glove into the stands. Why? he was asked. "Because it was pitching lousy," he replied. With new glove in tow, Murph threw shutout ball and two saves in his next two opportunities. For those who have front row seats, it's a good thing he's not a shot-putter after a bad put.

Still another Murphyism is recalled by NBC's Bob Costas, who tells of Murphy and three BoSox teammates walking to their hotel following a ballgame. Suddenly, the four strapping athletes happened upon a black cat, a recognized purveyor of bad luck. Murphy quickly jogged across the street, out of the feline's way, while the others kept walking, letting the black beast cross their path, and even uttering a few "kitty, kitty" purrs while laughing at Murph. The tag line to this occurrence was that Murphy went on to four consecutive saves in his next four outings, while his nonsuperstitious Red Sox mates, all pitchers, slumped severely . . . with one even being sent down to Pawtucket.

Brian Holton

Brian Holton, formerly with the Baltimore Orioles, may be a chapter by himself, as he readily admits to a wealth of superstitions and rituals he's compelled to adhere to and which he believes make him an effective pitcher (18 wins and a 3.45 ERA over 152 appearances in roughly three and a half years through 1989).

Holton begins his procedure in the clubhouse, getting dressed the same exact way before every game. He'll put on both of his right socks; then his two left socks; then his shorts; shirt; sleeves; pants; game jersey; his left spikes, tying them up to the next-to-last lace; then his right spikes with the same lacing scenario; then his hat; and finally his jacket, buttoning only the last three buttons.

He makes sure there are three cans of Copenhagen chewing tobacco in his right rear pocket, and a lasso in his left pocket. He'll wear a towel with the towel tag on the right side, and grab a cup of coffee.

Then Holton will walk by himself—if a teammate wants to walk with him, he'll stop and let the player go ahead of him—to the bull pen and sit in the same seat—in Baltimore, he had teammate Joe Price sitting to his left and fellow hurler Kevin Hickey to his right. During the game he'll sit with his elbows on his knees, his towel, jacket, and seat in exactly the same position.

When told to get up, he'll kick, spin around, and throw his warm-ups in the same order—each new inning, he'll throw four fastballs, four curves, two fastballs, five curves, and two fastballs.

When he takes the field, he'll get the ball in front of the mound and walk counterclockwise (noting third base, second base, and first base) onto the pitching rubber, sort of screwing himself into the hill, spinning four times to the right and then four times to the left. When he's ready for that first hitter, he'll set a foot on the rubber (left for a lefty hitter and right for a righty hitter) and then let the games begin.

With important situations on the line, Holton, who also eats spaghetti before every big game, will take the lasso from his pocket and rope a selected teammate's thumb. Jay Howell's thumb was the first he lassoed, in Los Angeles while both were with the Dodgers, and he targeted O's teammate Gregg Olson for lasso duty in Baltimore.

Holton said he would not let anything interfere with his preparation routine, but if something did, he'd be ready with Plan B. Said Holton, "I don't have a Plan B yet, but I'll think of one in a hurry."

[*Author's Note:* The O's tired of Holton's antics and released him in 1990. Odds are, he'll take his act on the road elsewhere in '91.]

Roger McDowell

Philadelphia Phillies reliever Roger McDowell, number 13 on his back, goes through this routine: He licks his hand, touches the button on his cap, touches the bill of his cap, wipes his fingers against each other, picks the ball out of his glove, rolls the ball in his hand, gets the sign from the catcher, wheels and deals . . .

Don Drysdale

Vin Scully, the golden-tongued voice of the Los Angeles Dodgers, said, "The Dodgers were always so properly taught—the behavior and the fundamentals—that there was little need for superstition."

Still, there are occasional slips even with the heroes of the game.

Number 53, the "Sidewinder," Hall-of-Fame right-hander Don Drysdale won 209 games as the workhorse of the Los Angeles Dodgers. Drysdale, a Van Nuys (California) High School graduate [*Author's note:* I also was graduated from Van Nuys, and thought it deserved a plug], was a hard-nosed player who didn't need good luck to intimidate his opponents. He'd just drill them. His oft-told philosophy: "If the opposing pitcher hit one of our guys, I hit two of theirs. If he hit two, I'd hit three. The plate was mine, and if a hitter dug in too close or too deeply, I'd stick one in his ear."

However, former teammate and current broadcaster for the San Francisco Giants, Ron Fairly, a 21-year Major Leaguer, tells of one Drysdale quirk. Fairly's nickname for

"Double D" was "Route 66," given for the circuitous route Drysdale took from the mound to the dugout after each inning. It seems that Drysdale was very conscious of where he walked and would not step on a bare spot in the infield. He made certain he walked only on grass, and sometimes the search for vegetation would take him several feet out of his way to the bench. At six feet five, 190 pounds, few would argue with Drysdale's quest for greener pastures on which to step.

Ron Fairly's own superstition, by the way, was this: "I always made sure I was at the ballpark on the first of the month and the fifteenth of the month. Those were the days we got paid."

Robin Roberts

Before there was a female sportscaster on ESPN named Robin Roberts, there was a Hall-of-Fame right-hander who toiled for 19 years, from 1948 to 1966, mostly with the Philadelphia Phillies, named Robin Roberts. The hurler won 286 games—20 or more for six straight seasons—and threw 45 shutouts, and he had a nervous routine on the mound that drove hitters to distraction, as did his pitches. Before each windup and delivery, Roberts would adjust his pants, brush his cap, tug at his pants again, and grab at his knee. This accomplished, he would zero in on the hitter.

Alvin Jackson

Former New York Mets starter Alvin Jackson, now an Orioles pitching coach, spent 10 years in the Majors and won 67 games (he lost 20 for the '62 Mets and 20 for the '65 Mets; he won 13 for New York in '63 and St. Louis in '66) and developed the following habits. He'd never walk on the double line (45-foot rule) to the left of first base; would always dress with his left sock first, then his right sock; and while in the bull pen at Shea Stadium, would line up nine cigarettes before each game and smoke one per inning until all nine were gone.

His major superstition was that he felt it was bad luck to strike out the first hitter he faced. He didn't mind giving up a hit and then striking out the side, but he had to get past that first hitter, and usually threw hittable pitches to him. When he did get a "K" on that lead-off hitter, Jackson would curse at the guy for ruining his game.

Bryan Harvey

Bryan Harvey, the reliable reliever for the California Angels (25 saves in 1989) goes through a set routine on the mound and in the pen. When on the hill, Harvey will receive the ball from the catcher while in front of the rubber, walk a half moon to the mound, and lick his fingers before each pitch.

While in the bull pen, Harvey will carefully lay out four sticks of gum, onto which he's wrapped a handful of chewing tobacco, roll it into a ball and pop the whole wad into his mouth. He'll chew it until the end of the third inning, then spit it out and head for the bathroom.

At the start of the fourth, Harvey will again lay out gum and tobacco, and then he'll chew it until the last out of the sixth. He'll hit the bathroom again, pop a third chew into his mouth, and work on it until he's either called to pitch or the game is over.

Whitey Ford

In the mold of Joe DiMaggio, perhaps no classier pitcher ever took the hill than "Slick," left-handed hurler Edward Charles "Whitey" Ford, the Hall-of-Fame World Series hero for the New York Yankees. During his 16-year career with the Yanks, Ford won 236 games, lost only 106, and had a winning percentage of .690 with an ERA of 2.75.

But Whitey didn't rely only on his talents—a sneaky-fast fastball, a wicked curve, and a deceptive pickoff move to first. He also relied on a bag of tricks that included some of the best spitters, mudballs, sweatballs, abrasion (cutting the spheroid with his ring) balls, and greaseballs in the Majors. Ford openly admits to making mud pies in the grass behind the pitchers' mound, then loading up while tying his shoelaces. In the 1963 World Series against the Dodgers, Ford said, "I used enough mud to build a dam."

But Ford's best "magic elixir" was a special formula of turpentine, baby oil, and rosin that he kept hidden in a deodorant bottle. He covered his body and uniform with the stuff before each game in much the same way former football wide receiver Fred Biletnikof would slather "stick-um" all over his hands and uni to make footballs stick to him like Velcro.

Jim "Mudcat" Grant

Before every starting assignment, Jim "Mudcat" Grant, the tricky right-hander from Lacoochee, Florida, who won 145 games with Cleveland, Minnesota (21 wins in 1965), and five other teams over 14 years, would spend up to half an hour rubbing a bar of soap all over his uniform. During the game, when he'd "wipe his sweat or dirt" off his pitching hand, he'd actually be loading up with soap—a variation of the spitter, mudder, Vaseline ball.

Grant reported that on one particularly hot day, his uniform began bubbling.

Other pitchers' rituals, habits, tricks, and nonconforming behavior included the following:

From New York Mets PR director Jay Horwitz comes the word that ace relief pitcher **John Franco** pays tribute to his late father, a former Department of Sanitation worker, by wearing a New York Department of Sanitation T-shirt under his uniform top.

Boston Red Sox reliever **Jeff Reardon** goes to the back of the mound to contemplate the situation at hand before he pitches to the first hitter he is to face. He also wears the same undershirt, spikes, and civilian clothing when he's doing well. He says it's a mental preparation necessary for him to pitch.

Cleveland Indians starter **Greg Swindell,** who chews his fingernails while he pitches, warms up by throwing three fastballs, a curve, and a change-up from the windup position, then goes to the stretch and fires a fastball before returning to the stretch to throw two more fastballs. Swindell also refuses to walk across the dirt to pick up a ball. He has to touch grass or let someone else get the ball and throw it to him.

Baltimore Orioles relief ace **Gregg Olson** only approaches the rubber from the first-base side of the mound.

Olson's O's teammate **Jeff Ballard** is a resin bag hurler, tossing it in the same location before each stint on the mound.

Paul "Bells" Miraballa, the reliever for the Orioles who fought his way back into The Show after pitching in the Senior League in Winter 1990, always wears the same undershirt from the West Palm Beach Tropics Senior League team that he says "got him back into the Bigs." He also stretches his arm, back, and shoulder in the same routine before he takes his warm-ups, and he won't chew any gum until he's called on to pitch.

Former New York Mets and Philadelphia Phillies reliever **Frank Edwin "Tug" McGraw** wiggled his fingers both at the plate and on the mound, before he was set to go into action.

The offbeat members of the **Baltimore Orioles** bull-pen staff kept a collection of Teenage Mutant Ninja Turtles in the pen for luck early in the 1990 season. Now pitching for the Orioles, relieving Donatello . . . Michelangelo.

Randy Myers, the Cincinnati Reds reliever who departed the New York Mets in 1989, brought his camouflage fatigues, plastic hand grenades, and *Soldier of Fortune* magazines with him to the Midwest and renamed the Reds' bull pen "The Nasty Boys." The macho-oriented hurler led the staff to a quick 1990 start, which saw them record an 8–0 mark, with 5 saves and a 1.86 ERA.

John Wyatt, a Kansas City A's pitcher, used Vaseline to doctor the ball. Before every game, in the thumb of his glove, he'd hide a syringe filled with the lubricant. When that hiding place was discovered by nosy opponents or umpires, he stuffed a tube of the gel in his mouth and squeezed some off when needed.

Bob Moose, a rookie pitcher for Pittsburgh in 1968, rubbed his pitching hand with pine tar and proceeded to throw a snail darter that easily fooled opposing batters.

Firpo Marberry's hat would fly off as he delivered his pitches homeward—an occurrence that happened with such regularity it became unnerving to hitters and a successful ritual for Marberry.

More recently, **Jim Bouton,** the New York Yankees' right-hander, employed the same hat-to-the-ground diversion in 1964.

Johnny Allen, the Yankees-Indians-Browns-Dodgers-Giants hurler from 1932 to 1944, with a temper as quick as his fastball, purposely tore the sleeves of his uniform, sweatshirt, and undershirt so they'd flap in the wind as he threw, distracting the hitter. When Allen was told by umpire Bill McGowan to cut his tattered sleeves, change shirts, or get thrown out of the game, the fiery pitcher left the field and went to the showers. For this, his manager, Ossie Vitt, fined him $250. Allen recouped the levy by selling his shirt to a Cleveland clothing store for $500.

Hey, if my pitcher wants to wear black underwear, or buy out the Frederick's of Hollywood catalog, and rub his body down with soap suds while he chews bubble gum and salami, grabbing unmentionable parts of his anatomy as he warms up while humming "Born in the USA," and can still win 20 or save 40, he can do it—or go through any routine he wants—and most Big League managers feel the same way.

5
Food and Drink

In the late '60s and early '70s, the pop culture echoed the words, "You are what you eat." Baseball players have been singing the virtues of certain foods for a century—and we're not talking health food here. We're talking good luck charms on a plate. Consider the success these players have had after chowing down on the comestibles of choice, the ritualistic victuals of victory.

Babe Ruth

George Herman "Babe" Ruth, the "Sultan of Swat," the "Bambino"—he might have been the greatest athlete the world has ever seen, considering what he accomplished despite what he put his body through. He was perhaps the best left-handed pitcher of his time—a winning percentage of .671, with 94 wins and only 46 losses, 2.28 ERA, and a 0.87 ERA in three World Series victories without a defeat. His prowess at the plate is legendary—600-foot home runs, 714 round-trippers in 22 years, a .342 career batting average with 2,211 RBIs. If his statistics were of mythic proportion, so were his appetites for food and sexual gratification. Given the amount of abuse he gave his body, Ruth's accomplishments loom even greater. But he was excessive. Los Angeles Dodger broadcaster Vin Scully describes him as "perhaps the biggest 'animal,' in all manners of the word, the game of baseball has ever seen."

A case in point might have been Ruth's rituals at the table.

Ruth felt that a mountain of food for breakfast prior to a game would give him strength and yield the best results. A typical Babe Ruth "Happy Meal" would include one 16-ounce porterhouse steak, six fried eggs, a full platter of fried potatoes, a pot of coffee, and a quart of rye whisky

mixed with White Rock ginger ale. Or, if he was out of town and wanted to cut down on his beef intake, he might simply sit in a restaurant and wolf down the following documented fare: an 18-egg omelette with three slices of ham, a half dozen slices of toast, and two bottles of beer, as well as his breakfast "juice" mixture of whisky and ginger ale. For dinner—for starters—he would consume a three-pound steak and a bottle of chili sauce, before he got down to serious business, which often included an entire capon, mounds of potatoes, spinach, corn, peas, beans, bread and butter, a whole pie, a quart of ice cream, and a small pitcher of coffee. And "Babe knows ribs." He loved barbecued ribs so much that he would often order hundreds of them from a restaurant in St. Louis and take them on the road with him. He often sold portions of the feast to his teammates, at 50 cents a pop, and provided free beer with which to wash them down.

Another typical Ruthian eating operation was his affinity for hot dogs and beer, leading to the "Great Bellyache of '25" (see chapter 6). And whenever Babe and his Yankees played the White Sox in Chicago, Babe knew that a meal was just across the street—at McCuddy's, a popular watering hole for athletes and journalists. Many was the time the Yanks and Chisox would play a doubleheader at Comisky Park, and during the break between games, while Ruth's mates would shower or grab some water, Babe would amble over to McCuddy's and order a dozen hot dogs and two or three (or four or five?) glasses of beer. He'd often slurp down the feast while joking with Ring Lardner or other writers who frequented the bar and grill and knew of Babe's habits. And several times, Babe had to duck behind the bar or behind other diner-drinkers to hide from manager Miller Huggins, who stormed in to find his overweight slugger and drag him by his ear back to the ballpark.

It has been documented that, on at least one occasion, Babe, nursing a hangover, asked the home plate umpire to thumb him from the game, whereupon the Bambino staggered across to McCuddy's to "recuperate" with a few tube steaks and a bucket of beer.

It was Ruth's expanding waistline, as it were, that caused the Yankees to change to the immortal and classic "Yankee pinstripes" on their uniforms. Yankee owner Col. Jacob Ruppert was embarrassed by Ruth's girth (he was fit at six-feet-two, 210–215 pounds, but often ballooned to

275) and ordered the attire change in an effort to make Babe look slimmer.

Lou Gehrig

Lou Gehrig, the endearing baseball immortal "Iron Man" for the New York Yankees, who played through injury and fatigue to record an astronomical record of 2,130 consecutive games on his way to 493 home runs, a .340 career batting average, and enshrinement in the Hall of Fame, was known for his love of his mother's homemade pickled eels. In fact, Lou would eat pickled eels whenever and wherever he could, not only because he liked them, but because he thought the slithery water babies gave him strength and vigor, and the ability to see and think more clearly.

Teammate Babe Ruth, with whom Gehrig later had a stormy relationship, was often invited, early in Lou's career, to the Gehrig home for dinner. Babe loved Mom Gehrig's cooking, and when he heard Lou swear by the healing powers of Mom's pickled eels, he decided to put them to the test. He convinced her to send jars of the stuff over to Yankee Stadium whenever she could. In fact, he had a standing order with her to send over one to three jars whenever the Yankees played a home doubleheader. Babe would spy Mom Gehrig sitting in the stands in the first game and then send the Bombers' batboy over to relieve her of the jar(s) of ambrosia. The batboy, then knowing what the Babe wanted, recipe in hand, would ready a feast for the slugger between games. Following the last out of the opener, Babe would head for the locker room and chow down on the "strength-giving" concoction of *Mom Gehrig's pickled eels and a pint of chocolate ice cream.* This gooey, gruesome mess would give Babe the strength he needed to give it his all in game two, and, as Waite Hoyt used to say, "allowed Babe to lead the league in belches, burps, and farts."

But it was Mom Gehrig's pickled eels that did it, and if Lou Gehrig were alive today, his smiling face would probably be gracing the jars or tins of some happy eel purveyor in every market in America.

Mickey Tettleton

Mickey Tettleton, the switch-hitting catcher for the Baltimore Orioles, enjoyed an All-Star year in 1989—26 home runs, 65 RBIs, and 21 doubles in only 117 games, while finishing with the AL's top fielding percentage among catchers.

And he and his wife, Sylvia, openly admitted that his good fortune began when his eating habits changed. He began eating Fruit Loops cereal every day for breakfast—and sometimes as a pregame meal—and he went on a home run tear. For that one season, at least, Tettleton swore by the sweet repast. In 1990, he left sugary cereal behind and took to wearing a Dick Tracy T-shirt under his uniform. The movie–comic strip shirt had been sent to Tettleton over the winter by a fan, and the O's receiver liked it and put it on. "I've got him out looking for hits," said Tettleton, whose first-half '90 wasn't as bountiful as his fruity '89.

Wade Boggs and Gaylord Perry

Wade Boggs is a card-carrying chickentarian. Believing there are hits in chicken, the .352-career slugger eats the bird seven days a week. He has hundreds of recipes to vary the fare—baked, broiled, barbecued, and sautéed; Italian style, Mexican, Oriental, and Middle Eastern.

Boggs, the perennial batting leader from Boston, has a twelve-day rotating chicken menu, and as he explained, "In the Minor Leagues, I could only afford three good meals a week, so I ate chicken—it's not expensive—four times a week. I won a Minor League batting title in 1981 with that diet, so I continued, and so has my hitting.

"While eating and following that routine, it adds to the positive ebb and flow of what goes on during the day, and I use it as part of my mental preparation for the game. It has a snowball effect, and two hits in a game builds to four over two games and five over three, etcetera.

"I believe, for me, there are hits in every chicken I eat."

But Gaylord Perry, a nemesis on the mound who threw legal and illegal (though he was never caught or suspended, the world knows Perry threw spitballs, Vaseline balls, K-Y Jelly balls, grease balls, resin balls, and scuff balls) pitches for three decades, covering 5,351 innings, also swore by a chicken diet.

Said Perry, simply, "There are outs in chicken, so I eat it and get outs."

As both Boggs and Perry were chicken eaters, Detroit Tigers announcer Ernie Harwell wonders, "If Boggs and Perry, both chicken eaters, faced each other in a crucial spot, . . . which one would chicken out first?"

Oscar "Spinach" Melillo

Oscar "Spinach" Melillo, in the days before Popeye, playing for the St. Louis Browns from 1926 to 1935 (he hit .306 in 1931), was a bouncy, five-foot-eight, 150-pound, sure-handed second baseman. He was such a sure fielder that when he spied Joe Cronin miscuing a ground ball in practice, he went up to the star and chided, "When you miss the ball, miss it like a pro. Always be aggressive and field like a pro." The advice helped turn Cronin into a perennial All-Star. But in addition to fielding, Melillo liked to eat . . . spinach. According to Ernie Harwell, Oscar (also nicknamed "Ski") was convinced that there were base hits in spinach.

"This was before Popeye," Harwell said, "and strength had nothing to do with it, but Melillo would eat spinach before every game if he could and was confident that he'd get hits as long as he ate the stuff." It is also rumored that "Ski" ate the vegetable as a doctor's prescription, to help eradicate a kidney ailment—Bright's Disease. At any rate, Melillo swore by the green victual and often had handfuls of the stuff in his locker to munch on before and after games.

A .260-career hitter, Melillo, who broke in with the Brownies at the age of 27, apparently went many a day without finding a good greengrocer, but that didn't stop the Chicago native from searching them out and downing a handful of leaves.

Ping Bodie

Frank Stephen "Ping" Bodie was an outfielder for the Chicago White Sox, Philadelphia A's, and New York Yankees from 1911 to 1921, compiling a .275 average in 1,049 games. The five-foot-eight-inch, 195-pounder was a roommate of Babe Ruth's for a time, but his prowess with the knife and fork outweighed his diamond accomplishments big time.

Born Francisco Stephen Pezzolo, Ping was born to eat, and he proved it one day in 1919 by challenging an ostrich named Percy to "the spaghetti-eating championship of the world."

The Yankees were engaged in spring training in Jacksonville, Florida, and Yankee co-owner Til Huston sponsored this eatathon, designed to win a few bets and give the Yanks some entertainment before they migrated north for the season.

Bodie consumed eleven huge platters of spaghetti, while the gorged bird quit at ten-and-a-half. With the ostrich lying bloated on the floor, Bodie heartily downed his last forkful of pasta and danced around the room as the king of the spaghetti-eating world.

Gates Brown

William James "Gates" Brown, a huge (five-foot-eleven, 220 pounds), muscular outfielder for the Detroit Tigers from 1963 to 1975, often sneaked into the clubhouse during a game to snack. Hot dogs with mustard and ketchup were his favorite energy provider, and as he knew that he would be called on a few innings later to pinch-hit, he casually, if surreptitiously, wolfed down his meal on the bench, figuring he had time before he would have to play. On one occasion in 1968, though, his manager, Mayo Smith, called on Brown earlier than the munching hitter had anticipated.

With a dog in each hand and one in his mouth, Brown had to grab a bat and hit. He stuffed the tube steaks in his jersey and stepped up to the plate in the sixth inning, with his Tigers losing to Cleveland 2–1. Concentrating on not letting the dogs fly out of his shirt, Brown lined a double to the gap, finishing up with a headfirst slide into second.

When he stood up, he saw that he had smashed hot dogs, mustard, and ketchup all over himself. Angry because he couldn't eat his hot dogs, Brown was made even angrier when Smith fined him one hundred dollars for eating on the bench.

Brown sighed. "I got a hit for you," he said, "and besides, I was hungry."

Dave Parker

Dave "Cobra" Parker, the six-foot-five, 240-pound mountain of a man who has spent 18 years in the Majors (Pittsburgh, Cincinnati, Oakland, Milwaukee) compiling a .293

career average with more than 320 homers, nearly 500 doubles, and more than 1,400 RBIs and who at one time was regarded by many as the best player in baseball, doesn't admit to having any rituals, habits, or superstitions, but concedes . . . "There is the gum."

Parker, now a dh with the Milwaukee Brewers, started the following routine when he was with the Oakland A's, as a means of getting prepared to bat without playing the field, as is a dh's standard method of operation.

Parker has his own personal gum and his own personal cup in which he puts his gum. He will sit on the bench, empty-mouthed, until it is time for him to bat. Then and only then will he break up four sticks of gum and put them in his cup. As he steps to the on-deck circle, he'll begin chewing the four sticks, which he has emptied from the cup into his mouth. He'll chew the gum while batting, and as soon as the at bat is over, he'll spit out the gum and remain empty-mouthed until his next at bat.

Dave chews 16 to 20 sticks of gum per game, and only when he's hitting.

Nice sugar rush, but through July 1990, he was among the American League leaders in hits, batting, and RBIs.

Steve Stone

Steve Stone, who managed 107 wins in 11 years for the Giants, White Sox, Cubs, and Orioles, from 1971 to 1981, and won 25 games in his Cy Young year of 1980, made food part of his pregame ritual.

When he was scheduled to pitch, Stone would stop at International House of Pancakes (his favorite pancake restaurant) and order and eat, precisely: two stacks of pancakes (total: eight), six slices of bacon, coffee, milk, orange juice, and sausage.

When that had digested long enough, he'd make his way

to the ballpark and stop at McDonald's for a milk shake.

It worked in 1980, but in 1981 he won only four games. Maybe the IHOP stopped putting a hop in his curve.

Nolan Ryan

The "King of K's," "the nonpareil of no-hitters," 300-game-winner Nolan Ryan often eats vanilla ice cream and chili beans to aid his digestive tract and to calm his nerves as a final meal before a big game.

Jim Palmer

Jim "Cakes" Palmer, the three-time Cy Young Award winner for the Baltimore Orioles, ate a large stack of pancakes before he blew out the Dodgers in the 1966 World Series and swore by the breakfast fare. He made it a point to wolf down a large stack or two of flapjacks before every start. The syrup or honey and carbohydrates probably offered quick energy and staying power and, more than that, gave Palmer the confidence he needed to knock on the Hall of Fame door with 268 wins in 19 years with the O's.

[*Author's note:* Palmer's nickname, Cakes, was given to him by his fellow Oriole players and may not have had anything to do with pan "cakes." He was probably tagged with it after his appearance in underwear commercials for Jockey, when players whistled and hooted, "Hey, Sweetcakes," at Palmer's near-bare derriere.]

Bert Blyleven

Bert Blyleven, who has won more than 270 games over a bright career, is a fun-loving hurler for the California Angels and has a superstition diet (or preparation diet, if you prefer) consisting of spaghetti and meatballs before each start . . . except in Boston.

When Blyleven is scheduled to pitch at Fenway Park, he will eat only spaghetti—no meatballs. He said, simply, "You have to have some superstitions . . . they are a means of focusing on what you have to do."

Greg Swindell

Greg Swindell, the six-foot-two, 215-pound Cleveland Indian left-handed fireballer (averaging nearly seven strike-outs every nine innings), bites off a different fingernail before each start and chews it through the entire game. He said he'd "never put tobacco in his mouth. Besides, it would ruin the taste of the fingernail." Swindell won 18 games in 1988, his only complete, non-injury season to date.

Jim Wynn

Jimmy "The Toy Cannon" Wynn, a smallish, five-foot-ten, 160-pound outfielder who bashed 291 homers during a 15-year career with Houston, Los Angeles, and Atlanta, said he got his power from honey, and ate jars of the stuff whenever possible.

Ron Kittle

Ron Kittle, Chicago White Sox, Yankees, and Orioles slugger (156 homers in his first eight years), ate nothing but eggs and corn bread during a 1982 Minor League streak in which he blasted eight home runs in eight consecutive games and finished the campaign with 50 homers in 127 games before being called up to the Sox roster.

Other food snippets:

Mike Cuellar (read more about this most superstitious of pitchers in chapters 2 and 4), the Baltimore Orioles hurler who won the Cy Young Award in 1969 and 185 games in 15 years, stopped by the same restaurant in Milwaukee and ordered several bowls of beef stew before each start he made against the Brewers. But elsewhere, Cuellar's routine was to eat Chinese food the night before he pitched. He deviated only when in Milwaukee.

Roger McDowell, the prankster reliever (closing in on 150 saves in six years) for the New York Mets and Philadelphia Phillies, typically stops by a McDonald's restaurant en route to the ballpark and orders two Quarter Pounders with cheese, one Big Mac, two cheeseburgers, one Filet of Fish, one large order of fries, one or two vanilla milk shakes, and one cherry pie. He said, "I need my strength if I'm going to have to wait until the ninth inning and then put out a rally."

The Baltimore Orioles' hulking slugger, **John "Boog" Powell,** a 17-year veteran who powered out 339 homers in 2,042 games, was a six-foot-four, 230- to 260-pound first baseman who helped lead the O's to five World Series appearances in six years and once gained 12 pounds in one day. After not eating or drinking for five days to make a weight clause in his contract, Powell celebrated by getting his strength back with two 20-ounce steaks, mountains of beans, and a loaf of bread. Later on, he ate another steak and, along the way, downed an estimated case of beer.

Frank "Hondo" Howard, the six-foot-seven, 250- to 270-pound Everest of an outfielder who played for the Los Angeles Dodgers, Washington Senators, and others during a 16-year career filled with 382 homers, would routinely down a half dozen hamburgers, three milk shakes, a half dozen orders of fries, a couple of pastries, and anything the fast-food joint had on special.

From SABR researcher Jim Skipper: **Harold "Pie" Traynor,** the

Hall-of-Fame third baseman for the Pittsburgh Pirates (.320 average over 17 years), got his nickname because of his love for pie. As a child, when told to go to the store to buy bread, milk, and necessities, Traynor always made certain he had enough money left over to buy some pie. When his youth team baseball coaches bought the kids ice cream after a game, Traynor always opted for pie instead. As an adult, rarely would he finish any day's eating without a customary slice (or several slices) of pie.

Mel "Wimpy" Harder, a six-foot-one, 195-pound hurler who pitched for 20 years for the Cleveland Indians (1928–1947), winning 223 games, got his nickname through his fanatical love and consumption of hamburgers. As he was seldom seen without a burger, he was likened to a popular cartoon character of the day, Wimpy, the mooching figure in the derby from the "Popeye" cartoon series.

Charlie Kerfield, the hefty, six-foot-six, 225- to 250-pound reliever (11–2 in 61 appearances in 1986 for the Houston Astros) who has eaten himself off a team more than once (Atlanta Braves in 1990), was caught on national television buying a couple of plates of spareribs while he was in the bull pen getting ready for an appearance in an Astros game.

Some out-of-the-ordinary dietary fare:

Pedro Borbon, former ace reliever of the Cincinnati Reds, of "Big Red Machine" fame (12 years, 69 wins, and 80 saves), once tried to eat an opponent's cap during a brawl, once threw a black cat at a catcher during a Winter League game in the Dominican Republic after thinking about eating the feline, and once bit a bouncer at a nightclub.

"Rookie Joe" Charboneau, a one-year-wonder for the Cleveland Indians in 1980, on one occasion ate five lit, filter-tip cigarettes on a bar dare. Charboneau; hardly the poster child for the Refined American Society, was known to open beer bottles with his eye socket, drink through his nose, eat fire, and chew bottles. Did it affect his career? In his rookie year he hit .283 and 23 homers. He was out of baseball two years later, batting only .214 with 2 homers.

Atlanta Braves second baseman **Glenn Hubbard,** a 13-year

pro with a solid .983 fielding percentage, once plucked a moth out of the night air and popped it into his mouth, gulping it down.

If former relief pitcher **Jim Kern** (13 years, 416 appearances, 88 saves for the Cleveland Indians, Texas Rangers, and others) reads this book, he might eat this page, as precedent has been set. He claims to have eaten the *Sporting News,* digested the notes taken during an interview by a sportswriter, and chunked down the last ten pages of a book being read on a plane by another writer.

Japan League legend **Brad "The Animal" Lesley** (a cup of coffee with the Milwaukee Brewers—parts of four years, one win, six saves), a relief wizard in the Far East who yelled like a caveman (or animal) before each pitch, often ate newspaper articles in which derogatory statements were made, and once threatened to eat the column's author.

Sid Fernandez, the pitching pride of Hawaii and the New York Mets (69 wins his first seven years, and the second lowest hits-to-innings ratio in baseball—Nolan Ryan is the all-time leader), wears number 50 to honor his home, the fiftieth state, and his favorite TV series, "Hawaii 5-0." He also puts mustard on his baked potatoes, rather than the standard butter, to shave pounds off his six-foot-one, 230-pound frame.

Ben MacDonald, the Baltimore Orioles' hard-throwing right-hander, at six feet seven, 212 pounds, was the number one draft pick in 1989, He apparently swears by mustard sardines, which he consumes by the can before every start—or at least every important start—in a ritual he began while pitching in college for Louisiana State, when he was named College Player of the Year. For his first start of 1990, in late July, MacDonald downed the fish and started strong, with a career of pitching and sardines looming large.

Luis Tiant, the Cuban-born cigar-smoking right-hander (229 wins in a 19-year career) with the turn-away delivery, ate nothing but chicken for an entire summer in the Minors. No superstition here—"chicken" was the only English word he knew, so that was all he could order.

Bill "Spaceman" Lee, the pitcher who was often in his own world, or at least in his own mind, admitted, perhaps as a joke and without any fact attached, that he ate organic buckwheat pancakes on which he sprinkled a half-ounce of marijuana.

America bought the story, as did baseball commissioner Bowie Kuhn, who fined Lee $250 for the admission. Lee instead donated $251 to an Eskimo charity. He said later that he had pitched under the influence of hashish, and many of his contemporaries had no reason to doubt it. Lee won 119 games over a stormy 14-year career with Boston and Montreal, but his behavior so disrupted teammates and managers that he seldom lived up to what was regarded as high potential.

Marijuana and hashish may have been small potatoes for **Dock Ellis,** another creatively minded hurler who pitched for the Pittsburgh Pirates, New York Yankees, and three other teams, from 1968 to 1979, while winning 138 games (19 in 1971).

Ellis admitted to being high on pep pills one night in 1974 when he tried to hit every batter in the Cincinnati Reds lineup. In the first inning alone, Ellis hit Pete Rose, Joe Morgan, and Dan Driessen, loading the bases. After walking Tony Perez, he came within inches of nailing Johnny Bench. He was pulled, but not before he gained a reputation as someone crazy . . . a pitcher with whom one shouldn't trifle.

He threw his best game on June 12, 1970, when, suffering from a sore arm, he fired a no-hitter for the Pirates against the San Diego Padres—while under the influence of LSD. According to Ellis, the field was "melting" around him. He couldn't find home plate—literally—and pleaded to come out of the game in the fifth inning. He won the game, 2–0, walking nine and hitting one and he could remember only bits of the game, but he completed a no-hitter nonetheless.

Ellis is also a trivia answer. He is the first Major Leaguer to wear hair curlers on a baseball field—at Wrigley Field, Chicago, in 1973—white curlers to keep his 'Fro intact.

Allan Peterson, a farmhand for the California Angels in the mid-eighties,once held a *Guiness Book of World Records* mark by scarfing down 20¾ hamburgers and buns in thirty minutes.

Baltimore Orioles' Bush League pitcher (no Major League experience) **Rick Rice** often ate frog legs before he pitched. He claimed, "It makes my fastball jump." Apparently it didn't jump far enough to leapfrog him into "The Show."

This food for thought, energy, performance, and concentration seems to have worked for some, shortened the careers for some, and added to the restaurant tabs of others. In all cases, the dietary habits of these baseball card heroes have become etched into the fabric that is the lore of the diamond.

Pickled eels and chocolate ice cream?

6
Freak Injuries

This chapter belongs in this book because it shows how odd (part of this book's title is "Oddities") it is for the world's greatest athletes to be felled by the most clumsy, weird, and luckless accidents imaginable. It proves that gifted physical specimens are just as frail as those fans who worship them, and just as awkward as those ungifted humans who revel in the diamond exploits of their heroes. This section recognizes that the legitimate wounds—pulled muscles, torn-up knees and blown-out elbows, blisters, rotator cuffs, bulging disks, and aching backs—are part of the game, but the ways in which these machines of human perfection were kept from playing are worthy of inspection. Also, we were a bit short, and this chapter was needed to satisfy my publisher.

[*Author's note:* The injuries are freaks . . . not the athletes who suffered them. Though in some cases, the situations in which the players put themselves certainly qualify the men as exhibiting freak behavior or at least questionable judgment.]

This chapter is dedicated to **Charley "Duke" Esper,** a five-foot-eleven, 185-pound lefty pitcher who won 102 games in nine years for six teams, between 1890 and 1898. It was Esper who incurred the wrath of his Baltimore teammates in 1895, who ridiculed him for "running like a lame horse." Newspaper accounts of the period indicate that Esper had a gait that resembled that of a man with a leg cramp. Ever since that time, any player who suffered a leg cramp has suffered a "charley horse."

In 1990, the Year of the Freak injury, we saw the following in the space of one week:

Ruben Sierra

The Texas Rangers' slugging outfielder Ruben Sierra suffered a badly sprained ankle on an elevator at a shopping mall. He slumped, going 5-for-48 following the shopping spree.

John Smiley

Pittsburgh Pirates lefty pitcher John Smiley broke his left hand when he slammed it in a taxi door (more taxis to come—1990 was also the Year of the Taxi).

Mackey Sasser, Dwight Gooden, and Tom O'Malley

New York Mets catcher Mackey Sasser accidently moved a metal chair on top of ace pitcher Dwight Gooden's left foot, breaking "Doc's" middle toe. Gooden was 2–3 at the time and pitched for several games with taped toes until he was healthy afoot. His season rapidly improved after the injury and was 8–5 at the All-Star break, 6–2 after the toe jamming. Need a chair, "Doc"?

And stay away from Mackey Sasser at all costs. The Mets' six-foot-one, 210-pound pariah filled their catching spot but nailed as many teammates as he did opposing base stealers. Three weeks after the Dwight Gooden chair caper, Sasser was taking batting practice when young, slugging first baseman Tom O'Malley knelt down to tie his shoe. Undaunted, Sasser took the next BP offering and lined a hard shot down the first-base line—WHAP—off O'Malley's head for a double. O'Malley was scratched from the day's game and had headaches for several days.

Nolan Ryan

The Texas Rangers' fireballer Nolan Ryan became the second pitcher to fall victim to a taxi in 1990 when Ryan, pitching coach Tom House, and House's wife, Karen, hailed a cab outside their Seattle hotel for a short ride to a health club, where Ryan was to partake in his usual off-day weight-lifting session. The female cab driver, apparently upset that the fare came to only $2.50, shoved open the passenger door just as Ryan reached to open it—jamming Ryan's right thumb.

"For a minute," said Ryan, "I thought it was broken." He pitched through the injury and never missed a turn because of it. One note: On his way to his three-hundredth career victory, Ryan also played with and through a stress fracture in his back by "thinking through the pain on every pitch."

Mariano Duncan

Another 1990 taxi victim was Cincinnati Reds infielder Mariano Duncan, who suffered a minor injury to his neck after the taxi in which he was riding was involved in a rear-end collision in Montreal.

Duncan, who was heading for the ballpark—Montreal's Olympic Stadium—was taken to a nearby hospital for X-rays. He missed several games and wore a neck brace (to protect sore neck muscles) to the ballpark for a few days.

Pascual Perez

The New York Yankees' enigmatic pitcher Pascual Perez escaped automotive injury when his 1990 BMW was damaged to the tune of five thousand dollars by a man who attacked Perez's vehicle in the Jackson Heights section of Queens, New York.

Perez was unhurt and could offer no explanation why the stranger, described by police as "some lulu," suddenly began kicking in the car's doors and fenders.

Kelly Gruber

In the first recorded incident of "parental fatigue," Toronto Blue Jays third baseman Kelly Gruber, enjoying his finest year in the Majors, begged out of the July 5 game versus the California Angels after attending the July 4, 1990, birth of his son, Kody. Gruber, his wife, Lynn, and son were all doing fine, but the elder Gruber was too drained to face fastballs and curves after experiencing life's miracle on Independence Day.

Chuck Finley

Also in 1990, California Angels left ace Chuck Finley missed a few starts after missing a few steps and spraining his left ankle—he can pitch; he just can't walk. This was reminiscent of his 1989 injury, when during a 16–9, 2.57 season, he strained the fourth toe on his left foot while warming up in the bull pen in Kansas City. He can face Brett and Wilson all right, just not his own bull pen catcher.

Glenallen Hill

The year 1990 saw rising young star Glenallen Hill, the powerfully built Toronto Blue Jays outfielder, miss a Saturday game (a 4–2 Toronto victory over, appropriately enough, the "City of Spiders," Cleveland) because he injured himself the night before while "trying to escape from imaginary spiders in a nightmare."

Hill said, "I have a phobia about spiders. In the nightmare I was trying to get away from spiders." While still asleep, he flailed away, kicked up and down, bounced out of bed and off a wall, and climbed up the 10 stairs in his Toronto condo, leaving a trail of blood as proof of his nocturnal bout with arachnophobia. He said, "When I woke up, I was on a couch, and my wife, Mika, was screaming, 'Honey, wake up!' "

On Saturday, Hill arrived at Toronto's Sky Dome on crutches following treatment at a hospital. After a stint in the trainer's room, it was reported that he had suffered abrasions, cuts on his toes and elbows, and carpet burns on his knees and elbows. Here's a six-foot-two, 210-pound 25-year-old who destroyed himself because of a dream. Hill was placed on the disabled list and missed more than two weeks' action after this "Freddy Krueger" attack.

Glenallen . . . next time, use a night-light.

Kevin Wickander

Another '90 boo-boo occurred when Cleveland Indians left-hander Kevin Wickander slipped on the Anaheim Stadium walkway, between the clubhouse and the bull pen, underneath the stands, before a ballgame. Wickander chipped a bone in his pitching elbow and spent more than two months recovering. The reliever said, "My cleats caught in a crack in the concrete; my legs went out from under me and I landed on my elbow." Bye-bye, season.

Jeff Brantley

Embroiled in a tight battle with the Cincinnati Reds for the NL West crown, the Giants relied heavily on reliever Jeff Brantley (1.72 ERA in 72 innings pitched by July 28). It was on July 28 that Brantley suffered the following injury.

During a simulated game, designed to give fielders, pitchers, and runners some extra practice, Brantley, the relief pitcher, was playing shortstop (reason and logic behind it unknown) and while going back into short left field to catch a fly ball, wrenched his back, forcing the hot reliever to spend the day in the hospital.

Some great starting pitching kept the injury's impact to a minimum for a while, but the Giants soon felt the strain, as did Brantley's back.

Too bad it wasn't a simulated injury. They could have taken him to a simulated hospital, where, after simulated treatment, he could have spent a few simulated days resting, without missing a real game.

Alfredo Griffin and Juan Samuel

A fight in a Pittsburgh bar, Chauncey's, kept Los Angeles Dodgers infielder Alfredo Griffin out for nearly a week with a cut-scratch-shiner above his left eye, inflicted upon him by the saloon's bouncer. Griffin was reportedly joking around and, when asked by a woman for an autograph, signed it "Jose Lind" (Pirates shortstop). An argument ensued between the woman and her date, who was enraged that Griffin had insulted them with the forgery. Griffin and teammate Juan Samuel apparently tried to intercede in the "domestic" dispute then taking place, and things got out of hand. The date shoved Griffin-Lind and things escalated from there. The bouncer, William Sturgeon—who was treated for multiple contusions and abrasions—jumped into the fray, and the Dodgers teed off on him, but not before he caught Griffin with a high, hard one. Griffin's eye was nearly swollen shut and remained sensitive to light for a week, while eye drops kept his vision blurry over the course of his treatment.

Maybe he should have signed the autograph: "Ozzie Smith."

And 1990 also saw Kansas City Royals outfielder-dh **Pat Tabler** struck in the head by a golf ball on July 10—the day of the All-Star game. X-rays showed no serious damage, but Tabler suffered headaches for the first few games after the mid-season break. On the same day, Royals' first baseman **Gerald Perry** suffered unexplained swelling in the little finger of his right hand. The cause was hypothesized (doctors sure had a handle on this one, by categorizing the culprit as being very unrelated circumstances) as either diet, sleeping wrong, jamming it somehow, or natural fluid retention.

Obviously, 1990 didn't have a corner on the weird injury market. Unexpected ailments have cropped up since baseball's beginnings. Some of the more notable ones include the following.

Joe DiMaggio

No one ever played the game with more grace and style and class than did the "Yankee Clipper," "Joltin' Joe" DiMaggio, Hall-of-Fame center fielder for the New York

Yankees from 1936 to 1951 (save 1943–45, when he was in military service), accumulating a .325 average, 361 homers, only 369 strikeouts, and two batting titles, while adding a new dimension to the way center field should be played. This entry proves that even the graceful superstars can suffer freak injuries. One such accident paved the way for Joe's sale to the Yankees.

In 1934, while playing in the Pacific Coast League for the San Francisco Seals, the 19-year-old outfielder was riding in a cab when his left foot fell asleep. Arriving at his destination, DiMag got out, put all his weight on the foot, and his knee buckled, resulting in torn cartilage. At the time, the Chicago Cubs were about to offer $75,000 for the kid's services, and the Yankees, Cardinals, A's, Giants, and Dodgers were also interested. All the other teams backed off after the injury, but the Yankees, cutting their offer to $25,000 for Joe D. and five other players, got his rights cheaply enough.

In his 1936 rookie season (.323, 29 homers, 125 RBIs), Joe missed the first 16 games of the year after burning his sore left foot by keeping it too long in a diathermy machine. No one had told him there was a limit on how long he should remain, and he thought the burning was part of the therapy. When DiMaggio finally played his first game in pinstripes, he smashed two singles and a triple in a Yankee victory.

Dale "Moose" Alexander

Another diathermy burn was suffered by six-foot-three, 210-pound slugger Dale Alexander of the Boston Red Sox. Alexander was a strapping kid from Tennessee who belted 25 homers as a rookie in 1929 for Detroit and 20 the following year, before being traded to Boston. His career average of .331 in five years (he won the AL batting title the year before he retired, with a .367 average) would have destined him for greatness had not his baseball journey ended prematurely with a stop in hot water.

On Memorial Day, 1933, his final year, the 30-year-old first baseman twisted his knee while playing at Philadelphia. He returned to the clubhouse and had diathermy treatment administered to his ailing joint. As with DiMaggio, the player knew little of this new treatment and thought it was supposed to burn a bit. When he got out of the tub, he had third-degree burns on his leg, which led to a gangrene infection. He almost lost his leg and was out of baseball by the end of the season.

Lou Skizas

Religion got the best of Lou "The Nervous Greek" Skizas, the five-foot-eleven, 175-pound outfielder for four teams during his four-year career, from 1956 to 1959. The slugger (30 homers in 239 games) always carried a large, Greek crucifix in his back pocket. Every once in a while, he would forget on which side he had placed the hard, sharp, metal object and slide on the wrong side, inflicting severe cuts on his buttocks.

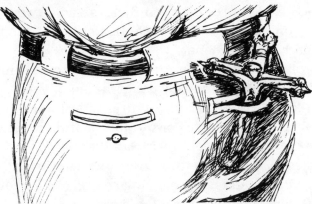

After a hard slide into third while playing for the White Sox in '59, players noticed a blood spot soaking through the seat of his baseball pants. When apprised of it, Skizas winced and said, "It's just my cross."

He must have figured we all have crosses to bear.

Graig Nettles

Graig Nettles, the golden-gloved, quick-tongued, durable third baseman, who hit homers and saved games with his glove for 22 years in the Bigs, was one player who would have been better off if there were no All-Star break. Twice during Nettles's celebrated career with the New York Yankees, he was felled during the three-day respite—and he was a six-time All-Star.

In 1979, Nettles interrupted a 20—home run season and broke a personal nine-consecutive-year streak during which he played in at least 150 games a year, by spending the break down in San Diego with his family. A day at home meant a day to do chores around the house. One of his jobs was to mow the lawn . . . simple enough for so dexterous an athlete. Graig, however, ran into an earthy difficulty, as the mower blades got stuck. No problem—he simply reached in to dislodge the offending twig and—SNAP-GRIND—three chopped fingers and a two-week vacation from diamond action. Nettles's glib reaction: "Next year, I'll hire a gardener."

The year 1980 saw the All-Star curse strike him again. This time, having hired a gardener, he happily took his wife and children to a Mexican restaurant for dinner. Little did he know that there were germs afoot. Within a week, there was an outbreak of hepatitis in San Diego—all victims having dined at the same ethnic Hispanic eaterie. Graig soon felt the effects, and his promising season (16 homers in 89 games) was shortened by a 67-game stay on the DL with the debilitating ailment. Stay home, Graig . . . or better yet, get away from home, far away, during the All-Star break.

One non-injury or oddity sidelight is Nettles's first name—Graig, perhaps the most often mispronounced and misspelled name in recent memory. When told by a fan that his child had changed his name from "Greg" to "Graig," Nettles, who once said of teammate Sparky Lyle, "He went from Cy Young to sayonara in one year," warned, "Don't do it . . . he's just asking for trouble. I got it, but I'm too old to change it. Tell him for me . . . don't."

Bobo Newsom

Louis Norman (Buck) "Bobo" Newsom was a much-traveled pitcher who played for 17 teams (some twice, some three times or more) during his colorful 20-year career, in which he won 211 games. The tough hurler shook off most injuries that were inflicted on him legitimately—line drives through the box that ricocheted off his feet, shins, arms, chest, and neck; and errant throws that clipped his ears, neck, and back—and his most infamous bout with pain ended with him gutting out a complete game, 1–0 victory.

Typical line-drive mishaps included the time Cleveland Indians outfielder Earl Averill, Sr., nearly crippled Newsom by lining one off his knee. Moments before, Newsom and Averill had been chiding each other. "Throw me outside and I'll knock you down," yelled Averill. "I'll throw outside and you won't come near it," replied Newsom. Bobo threw, Earl swung, and BOOM, the wicked liner broke Newsom's kneecap, sending the pitcher scrambling and crawling to gather the ball and throw Averill out. His teammates thought he was clowning, and they laughed. This enraged Newsom, who stayed in the game and completed a 5–4 loss. It was discovered later that his kneecap had been shattered, and he wore a cast for five weeks to prove it.

Newsom's most brutal injury, however, occurred on

Opening Day, 1936, when he was set to throw for the Washington Senators against the feared New York Yankees. As it was the season opener, the stands were packed and President Franklin Delano Roosevelt was there to throw out the first ball. In FDR's company were members of the U.S. Cabinet and the Supreme Court.

In the third inning, Newsom induced a Yankee hitter to ground slowly toward third. Washington third-sacker Ossie Bluege charged hard, bare-handed the ball, and slingshotted it toward first. Newsom, entranced by the great play, failed to duck, and watched intently as the sphere hurtled toward his face. SMACK. The throw struck Newsom below his ear, breaking his jaw with an audible crack.

He let out a yelp and began to run around in circles. He fell to the ground in a heap and was counted out . . . cold. Amazingly, he got up at the count of ten, refused to leave the game, and outdueled Lefty Gomez to win 1–0.

But Newsom's most colorful injuries occurred off the field. He once fell asleep at the wheel of his car while driving to Chicago from his home in South Carolina, drove off a Smokey Mountain road, and careened 225 feet down the mountain. This resulted in a broken leg and severe cuts and bruises. After spending two months recuperating, Newsom was ready to rejoin the Cubs. He stopped off at a mule auction on his way to Chicago, and as he bartered over a mule, the beast let fly with a healthy kick and nailed him in the same leg he had broken in the car crash. This resulted in another break and a lost season.

During his most successful season, a 21–5 year for the Detroit Tigers, Newsom once tripped in the dugout as he prepared to take the mound. He bounced on the concrete floor, wrenched his back, and blew two weeks of a brilliant season.

"Fat Freddie" Fitzsimmons

Freddie Fitzsimmons, a 19-year Major Leaguer who won 217 games for the New York Giants and Brooklyn Dodgers, fell victim to a chair in spring training of 1927, a 17–10 season for him. After consuming a typically huge meal, the five-foot-eleven, 185-pounder sat in his favorite rocking chair on the front porch of his team's hotel and engaged in conversation with teammates Rogers Hornsby and Bill Terry. The meal took its toll on Fitzsimmons, who fell asleep, snoring loudly, rocking in his sleep.

Soon the calm Miami night was shattered by the sound of a netherworldly scream. Terry and Hornsby thought Fitzsimmons was reacting to a nightmare, but they soon saw that the pitcher's right hand had flopped down and was caught between the floor and the rocking chair. The bruised hand was extricated, and the injury caused the Giants' star to miss four April starts. The mishap was costly, as New York fell two games short of a pennant . . . two games Fitzsimmons's replacements lost in April.

Nig Clarke

J. J. "Nig" Clarke, a five-foot-eight, 165-pound, Canadian-born catcher, who earned a footnote in the annals of diamond play by enjoying the greatest single offensive game in professional baseball history—an 8-for-8, eight-home-run performance in a single Texas League game: Corsicana versus Texarcana, June 15, 1902—also makes the odd injury list, due to love.

In late August 1908, playing for the Cleveland Indians, the 25-year-old receiver got married. He wanted some time off to see his new wife and asked his player-manager, Napoleon Lajoie, for a three-day pass. He reasoned he'd play better if he had the time off to be with his wife, and if he played better, the team would be better as a whole. The Indians were embroiled in a tight pennant struggle with the Detroit Tigers at the time, and Lajoie refused.

Clarke pouted, then went about his duties, warming up starting pitcher Addie Joss. Clarke caught two dozen of the mound ace's deliveries, then, when Joss was fairly warm and the velocity of his pitches was increasing, Clarke stuck his index finger straight into the hurler's next fastball. Stonefaced, he walked back to the bench, showed his bloodied, broken finger to Lajoie, and said, "I guess I can go home now, can't I?"

Clarke missed five weeks' action, and the Indians lost the pennant to the Tigers by half a game.

Waite Hoyt

Babe Ruth's best friend on the 1921–30 New York Yankees was Waite "The Schoolboy" Hoyt, who won 237 games during a 21-year career for eight teams. Hoyt suffered from a sore arm only once during the entire two-decade career, and that was as a result of a trip to a county fair in Pennsylvania with Ruth, Herb Pennock, and Joe Dugan. The four Major Leaguers lined up at a throwing booth—knock down a papier-mâché bottle pyramid with three throws—and quickly won most of the prizes offered. The carny boss, fearing insurmountable loss, asked the players to back up, which they did. They also began curving the ball, and eventually sent Pennock's wife, Esther, home

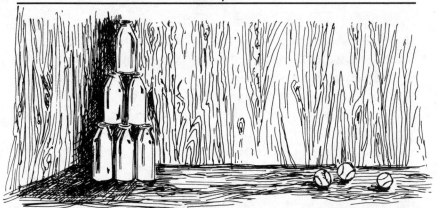

with nearly all the prizes in the booth—though they returned most of the prizes the next day. Hoyt woke up with a swollen arm and no strength. The ailing pitcher missed several weeks and lied to his manager by telling Miller Huggins he had hurt the wing on the field.

Jimmie Foxx

The Philadelphia Athletics' 25-year-old first baseman, Jimmie "Double X" Foxx, challenged Babe Ruth's sixty home run mark by belting 58 round-trippers in 1932. Foxx, powerfully built at six-feet-one, 195 pounds, might have hit more if he hadn't gone home after a game in mid-September and decided to do chores around the house. Replacing a lightbulb, the athletic Athletic fell off a stepladder and sprained his wrist. He didn't miss a game, but his once-powerful swing was weak for a week, and he fell short of the Babe's standard.

Babe Ruth

The Bambino makes this list by virtue of the "Famous Bellyache," aka "The Big Bellyache of 1925." The Babe's appetite finally got the better of him (see chapter 5), during spring training in 1925. Coming off a .378, 46 homer, 121 RBI season in 1924, in which he played in every game, the six-foot-two Ruth gained 60 pounds in the off-season, to bloat to over 270 pounds.

Still, he was off to his usual spring heroics, batting .447 despite running around all night downing booze and enjoying women. But stomach cramps soon overtook him, and a fever, as he prepared to play an exhibition in Asheville, North Carolina, on April 7. Ruth bellowed and collapsed on a train platform, and was sent back to New York. On the train there, Babe again collapsed and cracked his head on a washbasin. Arriving in New York, he was taken by ambulance to St. Vincent's Hospital.

The diagnosis was that Ruth was run-down, had influenza, and needed surgery for an intestinal abscess (unsubstantiated rumors of the day suggested that Babe was also being treated for a "severe case" of venereal disease).

Ruth came back in June but continued to abuse his body. Manager Miller Huggins caught him in a St. Louis bordello and fined him five thousand dollars for missing curfew. Ruth turned around and went back to his "house," leaving word that he didn't want to be disturbed until a decent hour, say 10 A.M.

The 1925 ledger: Ruth missed 55 games as his bulging belly dropped his stats to .290, 25 homers, and only 66 RBIs, as the Yankees, who went 89–63 in '24, slumped to a seventh-place finish at 69–85 in '25—their worst finish since 1913 and their lowest ending until their debacle of a season 41 years later, in 1966.

Belch.

On another note, one of the biggest rumors in baseball history, one that, if true, would have most certainly changed the fabric and historic destiny of the game, was Babe Ruth's "death" in 1920.

Ruth was driving his sports car on the outskirts of Philadelphia when he went off the road and flipped the car. Banner headlines around the country screamed, "Babe Ruth Dead in Car Crash." Reports of his death were greatly exaggerated, however, as the Bambino only suffered a banged knee. Later he confided, "It was a good thing I was drunk. I was so loose I didn't get hurt." Of course he failed to consider that his drinking was probably what caused the crash in the first place, but Ruth and his excesses survived that crash to reign over the sports world for another 28 years.

Lipman Pike

Lipman Pike was reputed to be the first Jewish player in professional baseball history and the first player in the Major Leagues to hit a home run, May 9, 1871. He played for the Troy Haymakers, St. Louis Brownstockings, Cincinnati Redstockings, the Lord Baltimores, and four other teams from 1871 to 1887, during the earliest days of the sport. He apparently missed a dozen games in 1878, when the five-foot-eight, 150-pound center fielder tripped on some jackets and caps while making a diving catch of a fly ball for Cincinnati. In those days, players left their gear lying around the field when they weren't using it. Pike injured his knee in the fall but came back to hit .324 before being traded to the Providence Grays.

[*Author's note:* That must have been some play, exhibiting a great deal of speed. Pike was a center fielder, and those carelessly strewn jackets were placed in foul territory along the foul line. He apparently covered quite a bit of ground before skidding to an injurious halt.]

Josh Gibson

All-time great Negro Leagues catcher Josh Gibson was one of the top power hitters in America from 1930, when he broke in with the Homestead Grays, until 1947, when he died at the age of thirty-five, before he was allowed to display his prowess in Major League baseball. He was known as "The Babe Ruth of the Black Leagues" and was the only player ever to hit a fair ball out of Yankee Stadium (in a 1934 doubleheader, hit right-handed, just inside the left-field foul pole). The six-foot-two, 230-pound catcher hit .474 with Homestead in 1943 and .398 in 1945 and he also suffered at least two offbeat injuries.

He was pelted in the eye, dead-on, by an errant billiard ball while playing pool in Mobile, Alabama, and missed two weeks with a closed, swollen eye and severely bruised eye socket as well, and one night in New Orleans he was assaulted by vicious guard dogs after allegedly running from a bordello—why he was running and how he encountered the dogs, along with other details of the incident, have not been revealed. The bites and scratches and bleeding, torn flesh on his legs and arms laid him up for only a day, though, as Gibson limped through the pain to play ball.

Mickey Tettleton

Baltimore's switch-hitting catcher Mickey Tettleton of Fruit Loops and Dick Tracy T-Shirt fame (see chapter 5), in 1986, opening the season as the Oakland A's starting catcher, was forced to the disabled list in May with a badly infected foot he suffered from tying his shoelaces too tight. Tettleton played in only 32 of Oakland's first 80 games due to the injury tie-in. He presumably keeps the laces looser now, as his 26-home run performance in 117 games in 1989 attests.

[*Author's note:* Though he missed 29 games following knee surgery that year, the injury was legitimate, occurring during a game against Texas.]

Eddie Waitkus

Eddie Waitkus was a better-than-average ballplayer who played in 1,140 games over 11 years with the Cubs, Phillies, and Orioles, from 1941 to 1955. The first baseman hit .285, struck out only 204 times in more than 4,200 at bats, and fielded his position well—a .903 lifetime percentage. But what makes Waitkus a baseball immortal was the injury he suffered in Chicago at the hands of a woman he didn't even know.

On a warm, calm night, June 14, 1949, Waitkus, playing for the Philadelphia Phillies and enjoying a .306 season, checked into the Edgewater Beach Hotel on Lake Shore Drive and prepared to relax and rest up for tomorrow's game against the Cubs. Little did he know that he was being stalked, by a woman named Ruth Ann Steinhagen, a 19-year-old who had, unbeknownst to Waitkus, become an Eddie Waitkus fanatic.

Steinhagen had built a shrine—filled with photos and news clippings—to Waitkus at her home in Chicago. And one more thing . . . she had recently purchased a second-hand .22-caliber rifle, which she took to the Edgewater earlier that day.

Steinhagen, who had checked into Room 1297-A under the name Ruth Ann Burns, sent a message to the front desk, to be forwarded to the ballplayer, which invited the good-looking bachelor to her room to "discuss something important." Around midnight, curiosity got the best of Waitkus, who knocked on the door of 1297-A to see what was so important.

Invited in, he exchanged pleasantries with the young woman, but without warning, she went to her closet, pulled out the weapon, and shot Eddie Waitkus in the chest. In a scene reminiscent of the one that took Roy Hobbs out of baseball in *The Natural,* Eddie was down . . . but not out. He missed the rest of the '49 season but came back the next year to play in all of Philadelphia's 154 games, as the "Whiz Kids" won the 1950 NL pennant.

Ruth Ann Steinhagen, who gave an "if I can't have him, no one can have him" reason for the shooting, served a few years in a mental hospital and was released. She never saw Waitkus again. He played several more years but suffered an everlasting injury in the incident. Prior to the shooting, Waitkus had been outgoing and trusting, but as time wore on, he became more sullen, suspicious, self-absorbed, and paranoid.

Lou Whitaker

Perennial All-Star second baseman "Sweet Lou" Whitaker, of the Detroit Tigers, saw more than a month of his season disappear following a back and hand injury, suffered on a dance floor. It was the first disco injury in Tiger history, as Whitaker apparently shook his booty in a manner the keystone sacker was not accustomed to. "Some dancers are tougher to avoid than incoming base runners," said Whitaker.

Willie Upshaw

Toronto slugger Willie Upshaw (now playing in Japan for the Daiei Hawks) once tore off his finger dunking an imaginary baseball—or basketball—on an awning.

Wade Boggs

Even .350 hitters have trouble. "Into" the Western wear craze of the mid-'80s, Boggs, the Boston Red Sox third baseman, liked cowboy boots. They proved his undoing when, on one occasion, in his hotel room in Toronto, he bruised his ribs trying to take his boots off. By Boggs's account, he lost his balance, fell over, banged his ribs against the arm of a couch, and hit the floor. He missed a week's worth of games, then played in pain for a couple of days before re-injuring his baby backs. It seems this second rib bruise occurred when Wade "hurt them by breathing."

Rich "Goose" Gossage

Fireballing San Diego reliever Rich "Goose" Gossage cut a finger on his pitching hand while eating a lobster. Goose went on to comment: "I was eating out of my range . . . I was going to order a cheeseburger, but my wife talked me into ordering a lobster." And Gossage helped blow the New York Yankees' 1979 pennant hopes by injuring his shoulder during a locker room scuffle with teammate catcher Cliff Johnson. Gossage started the Donnybrook by wadding up some tape and tossing it near Johnson. This led to some harmless but increasingly stinging banter between the two. Following a shower, they continued to trade insults, and Johnson heated things up with a playful tap to the back of Gossage's head. Goose didn't appreciate the contact and punched Johnson, who countered by throwing Gossage against the clubhouse wall. Gossage (six feet three, 180 pounds) and Johnson (six feet four, 215 pounds) exchanged about six punches each before teammates pried them apart. For their wrestling efforts, Gossage spent months on the DL for surgery to repair a torn ligament in his thumb and Johnson was dealt away. The heavily favored Yankees finished in fourth place.

Goose also suffered an embarrassing injury of another kind when, while sneezing one day in San Diego, he blew out his back—the result, five games off the field.

When injured, go see a doctor. That may be sound advice, but doctors err, too, and some medical sojourns have resulted in medical emergencies, as with the following.

Mickey Mantle

The New York Yankees' legendary switch-hitting center fielder Mickey Mantle, the king of pain and the leader of legitimate injury, fell victim to preventative medicine. In the Yankees' dream year, 1961, while embroiled in a battle with Roger Maris to break Babe Ruth's single-season home run record, Mantle heard of an influenza outbreak in the metropolitan area. Wanting to nip a potential crisis in the bud, Mick, on doctors' orders and the suggestion of manager Ralph Houk, went in for a flu shot. He beat the flu all right, but the shot caused an infection, and a silver dollar–sized abscess on his hip. This ailment kept Mick out of eight games, limited his output in half a dozen others, and cut his World Series activities to six at-bats, but he still finished with 54 homers, second to Maris's record-setting 61. On one occasion, Mick, with the bleeding, draining wound engulfing his leg, beat out an infield hit. Standing on first base, he was impervious to what was going on around him, but others gasped as they watched Mantle's pant leg fill up with blood. Rookie teammate Tom Tresh recalled, "I thought he'd been shot." Mantel was removed for a pinch runner, his abscess was patched up, and the legend of his toughness gained another chapter.

Another odd Mantle injury occurred on May 30, 1960 at Yankee Stadium, when Mickey, playing center field, caught a fly ball for the last out of a Yankee, Memorial Day doubleheader. As he turned to leave the field, some fifty thousand fans poured onto it, and soon the Mick was surrounded. The mob descended and Mantle tried to evade them. He couldn't. They grabbed at his uniform and tried to grab his glove. Mantle held on for dear life, but he did lose his cap, and as he bulled his way through this sea of unruly humanity, the fans got in their licks. He was belted in the jaw, scraped in the face, and bruised all over his torso.

Mantle finally got to safety in the clubhouse, and he remembers knocking down several of the marauding horde in the process. Still, it was Mantle who was on a liquid diet for several days, and who had to be protected by rope-wielding ushers for the next few games—to guard the idol of America against his adoring public.

Billy Martin

Mantle's longtime pal Billy Martin suffered at the tip of a doctor's needle, too. In 1985, while manager of the Yankees, Martin, beset with back spasms, went to Texas Rangers physician Dr. B. J. Mycoskie for a pain-relieving injection. The ensuing shot punctured Martin's lung and left the manager near death—and off the Yankee bench for a week.

Martin also suffered many fighting injuries during his brawling days, and one of these occurred during a run-in with Yankee pitcher Ed Whitson. Martin, who according to eyewitnesses had his arm broken during the melee, showed up at the ballpark the next day claiming he broke his wing while bowling. Billy always had trouble in alleys. Whitson, by the way, once injured himself while involved in the deadly maneuver of taking his sanitary socks off, thereby hurting his back.

Willie Wilson

During that brutal season of 1985, Dr. Mycoskie struck again when he injected Kansas City Royals outfielder Willie Wilson with penicillin to fight off a cold. An allergic reaction left Wilson out of the KC lineup for nearly three weeks. Thanks, Doc.

Ray Caldwell

Raymond Benjamin "Slim" Caldwell, an ace hurler for the New York Yankees, Boston Red Sox, and Cleveland Indians, winning 133 games from 1910 to 1921, was still a star on the Minor League level at the age of 43, when, in 1931, he went 19–7 for the Birmingham Barons

of the Southern Association. He beat Dizzy Dean 1–0 in the opening game of the Dixie Series, matching the Southern Association champ (Birmingham) against the Texas League winner (Houston) for that year. Caldwell was still pitching a decade later, even throwing an inning in the 1940 Ohio State League All-Star game.

Caldwell's entry into this book deals with nature. While on the mound for the Yankees one day in the early 1910s, Caldwell was well into the ballgame when the sky darkened. Raindrops began to fall, but the players continued and the umpire said, "Play on."

At one point late in the game, Caldwell went into his windup—as the rain fell steadily and the wind whipped around—and as he whirled and turned toward home plate, the sky brightened with a huge burst. A bolt of lightning hurtled from the heavens, and—CRACK—Caldwell was hit and thrown some 20 feet to the ground. The singed, burned hurler picked himself up, dusted himself off, and as players from both teams huddled around the electrified pitcher, Caldwell asked, "Was that last pitch a ball? Or a strike?" He remained in the game, but umpires called an end to the affair soon thereafter.

Snippets and cuts . . . more odd on-the-field injuries: New York Yankees Hall-of-Fame pitcher **Lefty "Goofy" Gomez,** who was as poor as a hitter as he was great as a pitcher,

tried to look cool at the plate, like his Bronx Bomber teammates, and used his bat to knock the dirt out of his spikes. As he began his cleaning swing one day, teammate **Frankie Crosetti** yelled, "Hey, Gomez," and Gomez turned as the swing continued, smacking him so hard on the ankle that he had to be carried off the field. He missed two starts.

Another Yankee Hall-of-Famer, catcher **Bill Dickey,** suffered the seventy-fourth injury to befall the 1948 New Yorkers, when, following the final out in a tough 5–3 victory over the second-place Boston Red Sox in the pennant clincher, the final day of the season, the then-coach jumped up, split his head open on the dugout roof, and was knocked unconscious.

Slugging outfielder **Kirk Gibson,** then with the Detroit Tigers, severely bruised his collarbone, causing him to miss several games, by following through on a swing and smacking himself with his bat.

Another Bengal, first baseman **Mike Laga,** viciously swung through a slow curve . . . and broke his wrist.

A third Tiger, infielder **Tom Brookens,** hit all right but didn't make it past his batting success. After belting a home run, he pulled a hamstring muscle while trotting around the bases.

Charlie Hough, knuckleballer for the Texas Rangers, once broke the little finger on his pitching hand by shaking hands with a friend.

Baltimore Orioles hurler **Jim Palmer** once pinched a nerve in his neck, causing him to miss a start. The accident occurred when Palmer, a 268-game winner, looked over at first base.

The Los Angeles Dodgers' durable second baseman **Steve Sax,** prior to his Yankee days, also "looked" bad one day. He re-injured an already sore knee by taking a pitch. He watched it go by and fell to the ground. Maybe he'd have been better off swinging. And on another occasion, Saxie smashed a home run and, while high-fiving third-base coach **Joe Amalfitano,** broke Amalfitano's thumb.

Strong and sturdy Dodger teammate **Pedro Guerrerro** strained his back after slugging a home run. Maybe he'd have been better off taking the pitch.

Chicago Cubs reliever **Ray Fontenot** bruised his ribs—and missed a week's work—when he fell on his way to the bull pen telephone. The call wasn't even for him.

George Case, a good-hitting outfielder (three .300 seasons, .282 career mark) for the Washington Senators, was sitting on the bench in 1947, nearing playing shape after recovering from a shoulder injury, when teammate **Bobo Newsom** came in from the mound and feeling friendly, pounded Case on the back, dislocating Case's shoulder and keeping him out indefinitely.

Boston Braves pitcher **Clarence "Climax" Blethen,** a 30-year-old rookie in 1923, wore false teeth and set them in his back pocket whenever he played. In a September game against the Detroit Tigers, Blethen was standing at first base following a single, when a teammate grounded a ball to short. The fielder scooped it up and flipped to second; Blethen slid in hard to break up the double play, forgetting that his teeth were in his sliding pattern. CHOMP, the teeth bit down on Blethen, who was out at second, and out of the game, as his bleeding buttocks had succumbed to his own teeth.

Chicago Cubs outfielder **Lou "The Mad Russian" Novikoff,** a decent hitter and exciting outfielder (he made every fly ball an adventure), had an all-consuming morbid fear of vines, or, to be accurate, a fear of contracting some ungodly disease from the vines. He played regularly at Wrigley Field, which has ivy and vines covering the walls. Afraid to pursue a ball near the crawling vegetation, Novikoff often let balls sail over his head and, on one occasion, stopped so abruptly, to keep from getting near a ball and the ivy, that he caught his spikes in the outfield grass and tore up his left knee, causing him to miss a week's worth of games in 1943.

Much-traveled relief fireman **Doug Corbett** broke his toe running to answer the bull pen phone. At least the call was for him, though he missed the assignment.

In a Rube Goldbergesque calamity at Wrigley Field in Chicago, Cubs moundsman **Ron Meredith** ventured too close to teammate **Dick Ruthven,** who was hitting fungoes, and was hit in the face by a backswing. Alertly, teammate infielder **Dave**

Owen ran to get the trainer, but in his haste, he misnavigated the dugout roof, clobbered his skull, and was knocked unconscious. The trainer rushed Meredith to the hospital, and all Owen got for his trouble was smelling salts . . . and a headache.

Dave "King Kong" Kingman, who had made his way to the Oakland A's—the eighth team for which he bombed home runs (442 in 16 years)—missed 11 games after suffering a knee injury that occurred when the six-foot-six, 210-pound dh turned at the plate to argue a called strike with the umpire. [*Author's note:* Kingman makes the trivia file as the only player ever to play for teams in all four divisions in one season: New York Mets (NL East), San Diego Padres (NL West), California Angels (AL West), and New York Yankees (AL East) in 1977.]

In Atlanta, with the Braves, light-hitting outfielder **Terry Harper,** at home plate, got caught up in the excitement of the game and frantically waved his arms like an out-of-control windmill to urge a teammate home from third. The run scored, and the six-foot-one, 195-pound Harper suffered a dislocated shoulder for his action.

In another vein, also with the Braves, then-coach **Russ Nixon** tried to hold up a runner at third, and pulled a calf muscle for his efforts.

Another Brave, catcher **Bruce Benedict,** yanked on his catchers' mitt during a stop in the action, pulled a neck muscle, and was forced to leave the game.

Infielder **Jerry Hairston** of the Chicago White Sox once extended his arms to pull on his baseball cap . . . and pulled a muscle in his neck: out a week.

Some out-of-the-ordinary off-the-field mishaps include the following:

Future Hall-of-Famer **George Brett,** of the Kansas City Royals, was watching the Baseball Game of The Week on TV one Saturday when he went into his kitchen to make a sandwich. Hurriedly playing chef, Brett ran back into the living room when he heard that Bill Buckner was set to bat. Buckner, being one of

Brett's favorite hitters to watch, was reason enough for careless-ness. Brett misnavigated a table leg, jammed his foot, broke his toe, and missed two weeks of diamond action.

In the locker room in New York one day, reserve infielder **Henry Cotto** was moments removed from a long stay on the disabled list as he prepared to clean out his ears with a Q-tip swab. The excavation had just begun when Yankee teammate Ken Griffey accidentally bumped into Cotto's arm, sending the cotton deep into Cotto's ear cavity, puncturing an eardrum.

SABR president Richard Topp tells the story of hurler **Reginald Bertrand "Jack" Powell,** who pitched two games for the St. Louis Browns in 1913. He was more widely known as one who traveled the vaudeville circuit billed as "The World's Fastest Eater." (This story may deal with food, but it *is* an injury story . . . trust me.) In a Memphis restaurant, on March 12, 1930, Powell, attempting to make some money and add to his gluttonous rep-utation, bet patrons he could eat one-half of an eight-ounce steak in one gulp, without chewing. With bets firmly in hand, Powell cut the huge piece of beef in half. He took his fork, picked up the meat, and shoved it in his throat. Powell had bitten off more than he could chew, and suffocation resulted. He was dead on arrival at a Memphis hospital less than thirty minutes later.

Another Richard Topp death story deals with wild Red Sox pitcher **Gordon Joseph "Big Train" McNaughton,** who man-aged a brief pitching career, playing for Boston in 1932 (0–1 in six games, with 22 walks in 21 innings). Ten years after his last Major League game, "Big Train" was caught in flagrante delicto by the husband of the woman with whom McNaughton was frat-ernizing. The husband saw nothing funny about the incident, raised a pistol, and shot McNaughton, killing him instantly.

One final look at death (from Topp) involves New York Yankee Hall-of-Fame manager **Miller Huggins.** Huggins, the nemesis of his outfielder Babe Ruth, led the Yanks to six pennants and, in 17 years at the helm of New York and the St. Louis Cardinals, won 1,413 games at a .556 clip. He died during the 1929 season while leading the Bronx Bombers for the twelfth straight year, at the age of 50. Cause of death: encephalitis. Cause of the encephalitis: Huggins had pimples on his cheek and inside his nose and apparently squeezed them too hard. An infection ensued and death overtook him in lightninglike fashion.

For more on the grisly subject of death, see "Odd Deaths" in chapter 8.

Moving on to lighter injuries . . . **Joe "Sandpaper" Niekro,** the knuckleballer of the Houston Astros, missed a start after burning his fingers at home during a cooking frenzy.

San Francisco fireman **Greg Minton** missed ten days of pitching duties after shoeing a horse and hammering a nail into his hand.

Another animal-related affair took Minor League great **Charles Columbus "Count" Campau** out of action. The five-foot-eleven, 160-pound outfielder who played from 1887 to 1905 (1,972 games and a .293 average) missed a handful of games while playing for New Orleans in 1894, when, while visiting a carnival, he slipped on some colorful and aromatic secretions left in the carny sawdust by a sick elephant, fell on his shoulder, and suffered a severe bruise and muscle spasms.

A fish took its toll on St. Louis Cardinals pitcher **Danny Cox.** Bill Valentine of the Arkansas Travelers recalled that while Cox was in spring training with the Cards in 1986, the six-foot-four, 215-pound righty took a day off from the Florida Grapefruit League season and went fishing. Going after a catch, Cox jumped off a low seawall, turned his ankle, and spent 21 days on the DL. He recovered to go 12–13 with a 2.90 ERA in 32 starts covering 222 innings.

Dennis Lamp is a fireman, but the Chicago White Sox should have called a real firefighter when Chisox receiver **Marc Hill** had his face burned one evening after teammate Lamp set Hill's beard on fire while lighting a cigarette.

The all-time no-hit, strikeout king, fireballer **Nolan Ryan,** at home in Texas with the Astros, returned after a day off at his ranch, with a sore arm from a rabies shot. Ryan needed the rabies shot because he had been bitten by a baby coyote earlier in the day.

Bob Ojeda, the starter-reliever for the Mets who was then with the BoSox, was stung by a bee during the playing of the national anthem. Ojeda was on the mound at the time and was scheduled to start the game. He did, got shellacked, and blamed the bee for the bombing.

Chicago Cubs outfielder **Jose Cardenal** begged out of the 1974 opening day's starting assignment because his eyelid was stuck shut. For a good fielder who stuck around for 18 years, Cardenal made a second career out of creative excuses. His most creative might have been in 1972, when he told his manager, Whitey Lockman, that he couldn't play because of "crickets." Incredulous, Lockman asked for further elucidation. Cardenal said his hotel room was full of crickets, and they made too much noise, interrupting his sleep. He was certainly too tired to play and blamed crickets for his demise.

Apparently liking Cardenal's stuck eye excuse, San Francisco Giant outfielder **Chris Brown** had to sit out five games due to injury. It seems, said Brown, "I slept on my eye wrong."

Another great excuse for missing a ballgame was given by St. Louis Cardinal pitcher **Charles "Flint" Rhem** in 1930. Rhem, a dependable right-handed hurler, disappeared during the middle of a tough series against the Dodgers, with whom the Cardinals, Giants, and Cubs were locked in a tight pennant struggle. Flint was nowhere to be found for more than 48 hours. Just as manager Gabby Street and GM Branch Rickey were about to call the police, Flint reappeared. He volunteered the following: Gangsters had kidnapped him, held him at gunpoint, and forced him to drink alcohol until he was dead drunk. This act, against his will, caused him to miss two days. Skeptically, Rickey bought his story and no disciplinary action was taken.

Getting back to the legitimate but strange . . . California Angels relief pitcher **Don Aase** suffered a Gooselike injury when he let fly with an off-the-field sneeze and separated cartilage in his rib cage.

Providing a sock-it-to-him injury, Atlanta Braves infielder

Randy Johnson sprained his thumb pulling off an offending foot warmer.

In a sock-it-to-me of a more violent kind, California Angels manager **Doug Rader** received a broken nose early in his playing career—he got it in the ring, as a boxer. Fighting under the name Lou D'Bardini, Rader had approximately 20 professional fights. According to Rader—tongue in cheek— he lost all 20.

Cleveland is no stranger to odd injuries. Pitcher **Jamie Easterly** pulled a groin muscle while watching television. Unlike George Brett, all Easterly did was sit there. He injured himself crossing his legs.

Another Tribe moundsman, **Ernie Camacho,** came up with a sore arm and missed a turn. His injury occurred, he said, while signing a hundred autographs, which was required by the team. Camacho earns another mention in this book for an operation he had in 1985 for the removal of bone chips from his elbow. The injury was legitimate all right, but following the procedure, Camacho hung onto the chips and now keeps them in a jar in his locker.

Camacho's writer's cramp excuse is but one of many injuries claimed by ballplayers who wished to beg out of a game. Several former teammates of **Fred Lynn,** when he was with the California Angels, accused the left-handed hitting outfielder of making up injuries whenever he had to face a tough lefty, and a few Yankees teammates of **Willie Randolph** tell of the second baseman saying, "I feel like I might pull my 'hammie' [hamstring] if I play tonight" rather than facing a tough righty. And there are plenty of cases on record of guys coming down with "the flu" or a muscle strain on precisely the night Nolan Ryan or "Doc" Gooden was to face them. But they all still pale by comparison to what follows.

More injuries occur in the home than anywhere else, and some baseball players have confirmed this.

Down for the count at home was Cincinnati pitcher **Ted Davidson,** who was shot in the chest by his estranged wife in 1967.

Davidson not only dropped the charges against his wife, but pitched that season for the Reds and went 1–0 in nine relief appearances covering 13 innings.

Also out at home were Los Angeles Dodgers outfielder **Ken Landreaux,** who sprained his knee getting up from a couch, and Detroit relief pitcher **Guillermo** [then known as "Willie"] **Hernandez,** who fell down the stairs at home and bruised his ribs. Fall number two on the same steps a year later resulted in a strained back.

Another back strain was suffered by St. Louis Cardinals outfielder **Tito Landrum** when he stood up from the dinner table. Landrum fell victim to weird injury on another occasion, hurting his wrist after falling out of a golf cart.

A third back sprain felled Los Angeles Dodger pitcher **Orel Hershiser,** who injured himself picking up his infant son.

Chicago White Sox hurler **Britt Burns** pulled a neck muscle—getting out of bed.

Vehicles are injurious, too, as former California Angels center fielder **Gary Pettis** found out when he strained shoulder muscles while adjusting the driver's seat in his Toyota. Chicago Cubs pitcher **Steve Trout** bruised his left shoulder—and missed a start—after falling off his bicycle, and rough, tough slugger **Gorman Thomas** of the Milwaukee Brewers injured his back while pulling himself out of a taxicab.

Yankee first baseman and free thinker **Joe Pepitone** suffered a musical knee injury aboard a bus in 1964, when New York manager **Yogi Berra** was enraged that utility infielder **Phil Linz** was playing his harmonica—"Mary Had a Little Lamb" was the offending ditty—following a doubleheader loss to the White Sox at Comisky Park. Berra told Linz to "knock it off." Linz didn't hear him and asked teammate Mickey Mantle what Berra had said. Mantle laughed and said, "Play it louder." So Linz did. Berra was incensed and slapped the harmonica out of Linz's hand and mouth. The small instrument flew across the bus and struck Pepitone on the knee, causing him to bleed. In mock pain, Pepi fell into the aisle. He shrugged off the injury; Linz was fined two hundred dollars and got a twenty thousand dollar endorsement contract from Hohner, the harmonica company. Berra was fired at the end of the season.

[*Author's note:* A Yankee first baseman of another era—and another degree of talent—the class act named **Don Mattingly,** has apparently taken up the harmonica. He carries it with him on road trips and plays it in his hotel room. Mattingly says it relaxes him. One wonders whether Yankee history will repeat itself, with another loss, a freak harmonica injury, and a fired manager— two of the three happen regularly.]

Nonvehicular mishaps have affected the likes of the following players:

Mark Bailey, Houston Astros catcher, injured his back and elbow slipping in a whirlpool (Jacuzzi).

The California Angels' slick-fielding second baseman **Bobby Grich** celebrated a million-dollar contract signing by going home to adjust his air conditioner. Picking up the unit, he suffered a herniated disc and virtually blew an entire season.

The Angels' million-dollar pitcher **Jim Barr** broke his right hand (pitching hand) in a fight during a 1979 pennant party.

And just so you don't think all baseball players are careless or thoughtless, whenever Philadelphia A's Hall-of-Fame pitcher **Robert Moses "Lefty" Grove** threw a tantrum—which was often—he punched a locker or watercooler or other ballplayer with his right hand—not his meal-ticket left hand. As Ted Williams once observed, "He's a careful tantrum thrower."

And a chapter on freak injury wouldn't be complete without at least one freak cure, no matter how bogus. Chicago Cubs trainer of the 1920s and '30s **Andy Lotshaw** had a "miracle" linament he would use on special occasions to help his pitchers overcome sore arms. Ailing hurlers who were unable to lift their arms above their heads would trudge to the trainer's table, and Lotshaw would pour out a small amount of the warm, sticky liquid. He would instruct the pitchers to rub this linament into their arms, and they could feel it tingling and going to work. Soon they were well enough to throw and win a ballgame. **Charlie Root,** a 201-

game winner from 1923 to 1941, asked Lotshaw for some extra, in case he felt more pain. Grudgingly, the trainer acceded to the veteran's wishes, and Root dutifully massaged in the liquid and told all who would listen that it and it alone prolonged his career for several years. Root's teammate from 1924 to 1931, **John Frederick "Sheriff" Blake** (no relation to the author), won 81 games in less than eight years with the Cubbies, and he, too, followed doctor's (or trainer's) orders and rubbed the mysterious cure-all into his ailing elbow. Blake was sure that this concoction helped him stay in baseball until his retirement in 1937. Lotshaw's secret linament remedy can now be revealed: It was nothing more than warm Coca-Cola. Coke may be "the real thing," but for Lotshaw, it was the "feel-good thing," along with some dime-store psychology, that repaired his staff for two decades.

So whenever you hurt yourself or feel clumsy following a particularly dumb maneuver, just throw back your head and laugh. "At least I can open my eyes, take off my boots, watch The Baseball Game of the Week without breaking my foot, and I got that Q-tip out of my ear before puncturing the eardrum."

7
Colorful Characters

Baseball is its players, and its cast of colorful characters is Americana in its purest form . . . also, I wanted to include these guys in the book and couldn't figure out where else to put them. So, for your entertainment, what follows is an ever-so-small smattering of some of the boys of summer who have made us laugh, cry, and scratch our heads with wonder.

And as so many other books have used their pages to sing the odd praises of such legendary colorful characters as Jimmy Piersall, Casey Stengel, Yogi Berra, Jay Johnstone, Al Hrabosky, and Sparky Lyle, all of whom were, indeed, colorful and entertaining, this tome acknowledges their achievements in the offbeat but chooses instead to inject new life with new tales of some oft-neglected characters who have added spice to the game.

[*Author's note:* Readers may notice that a number of the individuals mentioned here had a reliance on alcohol or that consumption of alcohol played a large part in some of the more offbeat events described here. We neither applaud nor condone the abuse of alcohol; nor do we make any value judgment whatsoever concerning imbibing. The stories are presented here for your entertainment and for the part they played in shaping the game we know and love as baseball.]

Now, put down your "WCTU" signs and enjoy yourself with stories of the players who follow.

Rube Waddell

If George Edward "Rube" Waddell's star burned bright—the pitcher had four straight 20-win seasons, six straight strikeout championships, and an ERA title—it went supernova quickly—13 years, 191 wins, and 50 shutouts. And Waddell himself was responsible for his own demise. Waddell lived every day to excess. His drinking and carousing binges were legendary.

More than that, Waddell marched to the tune of a different drummer. While playing with the Philadelphia A's, he would, on a whim, go AWOL to join a minstrel show, wrestle alligators, lead a marching band (throwing a baton 30 feet in the air and catching it as he marched), join a circus, or just disappear to engage in some behavior best left unprinted. Once, in 1900, while pitching for the Pittsburgh Pirates against the Brooklyn Dodgers, Waddell was supposed to start the game on the mound, but as game time approached and his teammates took the field, he was nowhere to be found. A search party scoured the ballpark and surrounding community and found Waddell, in his uniform, down the block, playing marbles with six neighborhood kids.

Drink often caused these spells of departure from the norm, and on one storied occasion, a drunken Rube boasted to teammates that he could fly. He bet on his success, and when the stakes were high enough, he stepped out of his hotel window, flapping his arms wildly. The next day, waking up in a hospital, Waddell yelled at his teammate, catcher Ossee Schreckengost, "Why didn't you stop me? I coulda been killed." His teammate retorted, "What? And lose the hundred dollars I bet against you?"

And it was Schreckengost, Waddell's roommate for a time, who demanded and received a unique contract clause. It seems that Waddell liked to eat in bed. He made sandwiches that consisted of two slices of rye bread, Limburger cheese, and sliced onions. The sight and smell drove "Schreck" nutty, but he could live with it. What dismayed him was that Waddell also devoured box upon box of Animal Crackers in bed, and "Schreck" said, "His munching keeps me up all night, and I can't sleep with all those crumbs on my sheets."

To please his catcher, Connie Mack, his manager, inked a clause in Rube Waddell's 1904 contract that specifically forbade the pitcher to eat crackers in bed. It became known as the "Animal Cracker contract."

However, Waddell's most flagrant act of bizarre behavior involved fires. Waddell had a grand fascination with fires and fire engines. Whenever he heard a siren, he stopped what he was doing and chased the vehicle to the blaze. Waddell was often spotted in fiery buildings, wearing a fireman's hat and carrying a hose, fighting the blaze with other firemen. But one day, Waddell's manager, all-business and no-nonsense Connie Mack, was at a loss when his star pitcher was on the hill. The count stood 2-and-2. There were two outs and one on in the second inning of a nothing-nothing game in early May. Waddell went into his windup and heard a fire engine siren bellowing in the distance. Without any warning, Rube gently dropped the ball on the mound and ran out of the ballpark to chase and fight the fire. He left behind a filled ballpark, bewildered players, and an empty mound.

When he returned two days later, it was, to him, as if the incident never happened. Mack soon tired of this and sent Rube packing, trading him to Pittsburgh despite his being the most (and I use this word only in the pitching success definition) reliable hurler on the staff—19–13 with a 2.15 ERA in 1907, before his trade in 1908. The old man loved Waddell's ability but couldn't take his colorful behavior.

Ozzie Guillen

The flashy Chicago White Sox shortstop, number 13 in your program but number one in your heart, Ozzie Guillen, is a young man who obviously enjoys life and likes to have fun. He plays hard-as-nails during a ballgame but relaxes with his own brand of humor whenever he's not making a play.

Before games, during batting practice, one of Guillen's favorite activities is to listen in on private conversations— teammates' and/or opponents' personal talks—then knock off someone's cap before running away.

As umpires are part of Guillen's audience, he uses them . . . as basketball hoops. Whenever he makes the last out of an inning, the shortstop changes from baseball player to basketball player and takes hook shots or jumpers, as the umps connect their hands to form a rim. It is said that Guillen excels from three-point range.

He has been spotted handing in lineup cards to games by pantomiming his lineup. If that doesn't draw enough laughter, he has been seen "moonwalking," using sign language on the men-in-blue's chests, and faking an anger attack by throwing his cap down, stomping on it, and walking away in a huff.

He has stolen bases . . . literally. During base change operations by the grounds keepers in Toronto and Milwaukee, Guillen has uprooted second base and hidden it somewhere in the ballpark. Bewildered grounds crews had to re-replace the bags.

During those secretive, strategic conferences on the mound between manager, pitcher, and catcher, Guillen will often intercede and utter some outlandish remark (e.g., to Carlton Fisk: "How can you catch when you're so ugly?") that will cause manager Jeff Torborg and the others to forget why they've called the mound meeting.

In a bit of a Bush League action—Major Leaguers seldom try to cheat or distract opponents by lying—Guillen has been known to shout instructions to fielders that don't exist and to fake taking throws or fake missing throws to catch an opponent off guard. He has also been known to be a nonstop talker to opponents, in a manner usually reserved for catchers and first basemen.

Steve Lyons

A teammate of Guillen's, ChiSox left-handed hitting infielder Steve "Psycho" Lyons must be considered "flashy" after what he pulled off July 16, 1990. While playing against the Detroit Tigers, he showed his grit by sliding headfirst into first base to beat out an infield hit in the fifth inning. The slide left Lyons with pants full of dirt and dust, and it became uncomfortable.

Relief was the better part of valor for Lyons as he absentmindedly unbuckled his belt, dropped his pants, and brushed away the dirt . . . forgetting that a ballparkful of fans was watching his every move.

Lyons was struck with reality, realized his faux pas, and quickly raised his pants, but not before revealing his white long johns to the crowd.

Others who have been caught up in the game, and failed to notice there was a crowd on hand as they stripped, include the Milwaukee Brewers' infielder Jim Gantner, in a situation similar to that of Lyons'; the Detroit Tigers' pitcher Mark "The Bird" Fidrych, who, in the bull pen as he was unexpectedly called into the game, removed his pants and put in his cup; Texas Rangers reliever Sparky Lyle, who, in 1979, did a striptease in the bull pen for fans who, on the last day of the season, wanted some of Sparky's clothing to remember him by (he wound up wearing only his jockstrap and a T-shirt); and, during a workout, Philadelphia Phillies third baseman Mike Schmidt, who stripped as a joke for teammates.

Mark "The Bird" Fidrych

Dropped pants were just one of the items that left Detroit Tigers phenom Mark "The Bird" Fidrych ingrained in baseball lore as a delightful supernova who burned out too soon.

Pitching for the Tigers, Fidrych talked to the ball and patted the mound (see chapter 4), cleaned off the pitcher's rubber, set up a car wash in the parking lot of the Tigers' spring training site, and celebrated his making the team by bringing a girl onto the field and having intercourse with her at his place of business—the pitcher's mound.

As a big-timer (1976: 19 wins, 9 losses) and on his way out (1980: 2 wins, 3 losses), he was the same man . . . a bit immature but fun-loving, and never egocentric, a nice guy to be around and to have on the team.

Injuries forced his all-too-early departure from the game.

His final failure to come back was not so much from injury as it was from confusion. During his many rehabilitations, coaches and therapists convinced Fidrych to change his motion, his delivery, and his mechanics. When finally his body was well enough to allow him to perform, he forgot how. His motion and mechanics were no longer his, and the fluid perfection that had blasted him to fame was not even a memory at this point.

He was a cheerleader on the field, in the dugout, and off the field, and his innocence made him the darling of America for one year (1976) and part of the next. His style— long curls bobbing up and down, a gangly appearance that made him seem like all arms and legs—and his resemblance to Big Bird, of "Sesame Street" fame, make Mark "The Bird" Fidrych a one-year wonder worthy of remembering at least one more time.

Paul "Big Poison" Waner

Paul Glee "P.G." Waner was a five-foot-eight-and-one-half-inch natural hitter with the Pittsburgh Pirates and three other clubs from 1926 to 1945, during which time the Hall-of-Fame outfielder maintained a .333 career mark in 2,549 games, with 1,091 walks and only 376 strikeouts (good eyesight). P.G. was an extremely heavy drinker who even drank on the bench (a handy flask in his hip pocket). He liked to say that a shot of whiskey was like mother's milk to him. Still, his manager and friend, Pie Traynor, was concerned about his excessive use of alcohol and convinced him to slow down—cut out the hard stuff and, instead, only have an occasional beer.

Waner complied and proceeded to have a horrible 1938 season—he finished at .280, 74 points below his 1937 mark of .354. Realizing this, Traynor talked Waner into accompanying him on a walk to the ballpark prior to a game. He suggested that the pair stop for a quick one in a neighborhood saloon, and when Waner ordered a beer, Traynor stopped him and ordered him a couple of shots of whiskey instead. Suitably fueled up, Waner went on to have a typically solid season the rest of the way . . . and he rebounded to hit .328 in 1939.

On another binge, reported by *St. Louis Post-Dispatch* sportswriter Bob Broeg, Waner stepped into his favorite

St. Louis saloon, owned by former player Heinie Meine. (Known as "The Count of Luxemburg," Meine, a St. Louis native, pitched for the Cardinals and Pirates from 1922 to 1934—a 66–50 record in 999 innings.)

Meine treated Waner well, and the outfielder, after the "rough" night, staggered into the ballpark with an obvious hangover. St. Louis manager Gabby Street saw this and gleefully gave the information to his starting pitcher, Jerome "Dizzy" Dean. Street yelled, "P.G. is so drunk and hung over, he can't see."

As Waner usually hit Ol' Diz pretty well, Dean was overjoyed. "Oh, God, I've got him today," said Diz.

Waner went out and hit four doubles against Dean, going 4-for-4.

Hack Wilson

Lewis Robert "Hack" Wilson was a five-foot-six, 190-pound slugging outfielder for the New York Giants, Chicago Cubs, and Brooklyn Dodgers from 1923 to 1934. He amassed 244 homers and a .307 average during his career, and in his heyday, 1930 with Chicago, he smashed 56 home runs and a Major League record 190 RBIs. And one more thing, Wilson really liked to drink. It was often said that more alcohol than blood flowed through his veins.

In an oft-told tale, recently recalled by Bob Broeg, Hack was playing for Joe McCarthy's Cubbies in 1928 when McCarthy discovered matchboxes from about a dozen speakeasies in Wilson's locker. Fearing that his slugging outfielder could hurt himself by drinking rotgut gin—Wilson also kept a flask of lighter fluid–like gin on his person at all times—McCarthy decided to talk Wilson out of the hard stuff by enlisting the help of his grounds keeper.

Summoning Wilson into his office, McCarthy lectured

his outfielder on the danger of drinking gin, suggesting he move down to beer or something with a higher water content. He told the player, "Do you see this worm that the grounds keeper brought in?"

Wilson nodded.

McCarthy poured a glass of water from a watercooler in his office and placed the worm in it. The *vermis* joyfully swam around the clear liquid.

Then McCarthy asked for Wilson's flask and poured from it a half a glass of gin.

He took the happy night crawler out of the water and put it in the gin. The two men watched as the insect immediately shriveled up and died.

McCarthy handed the glass of gin-and-worm to Wilson and asked, "Now do you understand what I've been trying to tell you?"

The outfielder thought for a moment and smiled, "Thanks, a lot, Skip. I get it. If I drink gin, I won't get worms."

"Boom Boom" Beck

Walter "Boom Boom" Beck was a teammate of Hack Wilson's when both played for the Brooklyn Dodgers, managed by Casey Stengel in 1934. Beck was a flaky right-hander (six feet two, 200 pounds), who lasted 12 years for six teams despite a 38–69 mark and 4.30 ERA.

Red Patterson, the former sportswriter and Dodgers, Yankees, Angels exec, remembered a special story involving Beck and Wilson while both toiled for Brooklyn in 1934.

Beck was having a terrible season (2–6 with a 7.42 ERA) while Wilson, in his final season, hit .245 with only six homers. They were typical of the '34 Dodgers, who finished 71–81, 23½ games behind the Cardinals.

It was a hot July 4th, and Beck was on the hill against

Philadelphia in the old Baker Bowl ballpark. He was getting pummeled by the Phils, who had a worse record than did the Bums.

The Dodger manager came out to talk to Beck, who had given up shot after shot against the tinny right-field wall. Those bullets, through, around and over Hack Wilson, had made resounding BOOM sounds, which forever gave Beck his nickname.

When Casey came out to take the ball from Beck and tell him he was through, Beck just stared in the direction of the aging outfielder.

Wilson, meanwhile, was nursing a hangover, and used this break in the action to bend over, put his hands on his knees, and watch the sweat drop off his forehead and onto the grass. Lost in thought and stupor, Wilson was impervious to the action on the mound, some 250 feet away.

Stengel asked for the ball, and Beck blew his top. He reared back and fired the ball over Wilson's head and against the tin wall.

CLANG. The ball ricocheted off the right-field barrier. Wilson cursed. He thought someone had hit it past him again. He turned, fielded the ball cleanly off the wall, whirled, and fired a perfect strike to second base.

While all the players and fans in attendance began to laugh, Wilson was in no mood to be a joke's victim. He lumbered in and chased Beck off the field, into the dugout, and out into the street.

Both Beck and Wilson were gone before next season.

Bob O'Farrell

Bob O'Farrell was a 21-year catcher for the Cubs, Cardinals, and Giants, from 1915 to 1935. A solid receiver and tough-out contact hitter, O'Farrell had a sloppy habit of spitting tobacco juice on the shoes of opposing hitters as they dug in at the plate. One day, in 1915, with chaw firmly in his mouth, O'Farrell expectorated. This time he chose the wrong shoes—those of George Albert "Lefty" Tyler, a pitcher for the Boston Braves. In a 12-year career that also took him to Chicago to play with the Cubs, Tyler finished with 127 wins and a credible 1,003 strikeouts—and he could throw hard. With O'Farrell spitting on his feet, Tyler, angered over his juicy spikes, grabbed a ball and hit O'Farrell in the throat with it. A fight ensued, and O'Farrell was at least temporarily cured of using opposing players as his personal spittoons.

O'Farrell had another endearing habit—that is, if you're a male chauvinist. He utilized an orthodontic feature—a gap between his two front teeth—by spitting things through it . . . and he apparently had great aim. In addition to tobacco juice, O'Farrell loved to fill his mouth with BBs (rifle shot) and pop a few at the breasts of women whenever and wherever he found them—usually in the front rows at the ballpark. In today's world, he'd have made a great poster boy for the National Organization of Women, but 70 years ago, he was simply labeled a "scamp."

Lou Piniella

Lou Piniella, the manager of the Cincinnati Reds, led a solid 18-year career as a hitter-outfielder for the New York Yankees, during which time the clutch-hitting "Sweet Lou" hit .291 (seven .300 seasons), with 102 homers, a .305 ALCS average, and a .319 World Series mark.

Lou Piniella was and is a hard worker. No one ever accused him of not giving it his all. But then again, no one ever rewarded him for being able to control his temper either. Piniella's temper was legendary, and broken watercoolers and bashed-in walls and lockers were run-of-the-mill around American League clubhouses from 1964 to 1984.

One of Piniella's most humorous displays was remembered by his teammate on the Portland Beavers of the PCL in 1967, hot-hitting Richie Scheinblum (an eight-year Major Leaguer, three-time .300 hitter), later a teammate with Cleveland and again with Kansas City.

Scheinblum recalled that the Beavers were playing a home game in Portland when the team owner made a special trip to the clubhouse before the game. He explained to the players that some nuns, special guests and relatives of his, were sitting in the VIP seats, right next to the Beavers' dugout. The owner asked the players to watch their language and make a special effort to be kind and considerate. Lou nodded and tried.

In the first inning, Piniella struck out. Angry, he was about to slam the bat down when he remembered the nuns. Being a gentleman, he smiled, placed his bat gently in the bat rack, and sat down.

In the fourth inning, Piniella saw his pitch but missed getting it and popped up weakly to second. Again he was angry, but again he contained himself and sat down on the bench.

In the seventh, Piniella was again a strikeout victim, and this time he was enraged. He glanced over at the nuns and walked hurriedly to the bench. He slammed his bat in the bat rack and hurled himself down on the bench.

The rage was growing.

In the ninth inning, with the game on the line and the tying run on, Piniella again got his pitch and again missed taking advantage of it. He fouled it off, only to strike out on the next delivery.

He slowly walked to the bat rack and gently placed his bat in it. He walked over to the nuns and smiled. He pressed his nose and lips against the screen and was now face to face with the religious ladies.

Holding back no longer, Piniella let fly, with all the force and might his voice box would allow, with a string of the loudest, most vulgar, most creative epithets ever heard on a baseball field.

Relieved, he smiled and walked to the clubhouse. Shocked, the nuns sat speechless.

Unburdened, Piniella went 4-for-4 the next day and was soon called up to the Majors to begin his long career in the Bigs.

Lou "The Mad Russian" Novikoff

A player who was the embodiment of long-suffering Chicago Cubs fans was Lou Novikoff, a five-year Major Leaguer (Cubs and Phillies) from 1941 to 1946, who hit a solid .282 and played an adventurous outfield. As discussed in chapter 6, "Freak Injuries," Novikoff had a mortal fear of vines and of catching diseases from vines. This proved to be a tough nut to crack, considering that his home ballpark, Wrigley Field in Chicago, as well as Forbes Field in Pittsburgh, had vine-covered outfield walls, which were within a few feet of Novikoff.

He came to the Majors amid much hype and promise, after hitting .367, .368, and .363 during his last three Minor League seasons, belting 23 triples one year and 41 homers another. But his fielding was a liability.

Novikoff put up those Minor League numbers by being a free swinger—hitting any pitch that dared to be close—but once in the Majors, he figured that he must be selective. His hitting suffered, and as a result, Cubs owner Phillip K.

Wrigley invoked one of the stranger contract clauses in the game.

He awarded Novikoff a five dollar bonus every time he struck out swinging. It worked to the extent that he raised his average to .300 his second season, but it failed in that he often went hunting for high pitches in crucial situations when a walk could mean a run, causing teammates and coaches to bark, "You short of money, Lou?"

In one of the oddest superstitions in baseball lore, Novikoff insisted that his wife, Esther, ridicule him, rag on him, and ride him from the stands. Novikoff said the taunts inspired him to play better baseball.

Without his wife to yell at him, Novikoff hit a meager .241 in his rookie season. He brought his love with him the next year, and she yelled her way and his way to a .300 sophomore season—yelling and five dollars per swinging "K" did the trick.

When there was no one to yell at him, Novikoff went to music for luck. He sang whenever he got the urge, and that often occurred at the oddest times—during a ballgame, up at the plate, in a shower in the locker room, on a train in the middle of the night, or in his hotel room at dawn.

He once broke curfew to sing at a nightclub, and when his manager, Charlie Grimm, heard the rendition on the radio, Grimm grabbed a taxi and made it to the nightclub just in time for Novikoff's closing number. Grimm applauded and went up to his curfew-violating outfielder, fining him on the spot.

Novikoff paid the fine, but not until after he claimed he only did it for luck . . . to help the Cubs win.

Thanks for the laughs, the thrills, and the different approach to baseball, guys.

8
Oddities

This chapter contains little bits of information included for your entertainment—the side factors that make baseball and its players a microcosm of Americana unparalleled by any other cross-section of society.

These tidbits of baseball lore don't fit in anywhere else in this book, but we would be remiss if we didn't include them.

Germany Schaefer

The only man to steal first base was Herman A. "Germany" Schaefer, a fun-loving and colorful infielder who played for the Detroit Tigers, Washington Senators, and four other teams from 1901 to 1918 while hitting .257 and stealing 201 bases.

In a 1908 game between Schaefer's Detroit Tigers and the Cleveland Indians, Schaefer, at first with another runner at third, stole second as part of an attempted double steal with the lead runner breaking for the plate. The Cleveland catcher held onto the ball, forcing the runner at third to hold his ground.

Schaefer, known for his sense of humor, said, "Let's try that again," and on the next pitch, ran back to first base. Never faced with that situation before, the umpires did not know how to call it and allowed Schaefer to remain on first.

On the following pitch, Schaefer again broke for second, and this time he drew a throw from the catcher. Schaefer was safe at second and the run scored. The strategy worked.

The league office, afraid that this type of maneuver would make a mockery of the game, instructed umpires to eject any runner who ran the bases in a reverse order.

Schaefer's steal of first will never be duplicated.

Gaylord Perry

Gaylord Jackson Perry, the spitball-throwing Hall-of-Fame candidate with 314 wins and 3,535 strikeouts over a 22-year career for eight teams, was said to have one of the worst swings in baseball when he first came up with the San Francisco Giants in 1962.

His manager that year, Alvin Dark, said of Perry, "We'll put a man on the moon before Perry will ever hit a homer." In 1962 the idea of Americans on the moon was simply a gleam in the eye of President John F. Kennedy.

On July 20, 1969, shortly after Apollo 11 touched down on the moon, Gaylord Perry hit his first career home run, after nearly five hundred at bats. Perry finished his career with six home runs in 1,076 at bats, and, to date, the

United States has made six manned lunar landings, one for each of Perry's clouts.

Roseanne Barr and Our National Anthem

Roseanne Barr, the irreverent comedienne and star of the "Roseanne" TV show, made baseball infamy on July 26, 1990, when she was invited to sing the national anthem prior to a game between the San Diego Padres and the Cincinnati Reds at Jack Murphy Stadium, San Diego.

Barr, invited by new Padres owner (chairman and managing partner) Tom Werner, who is executive producer and co-creator of "Roseanne," thought it was a good idea at the time.

She turned the pregame ritual into a loud boo-fest when she gave a shrill rendition of "The Star Spangled Banner." Barr sang it quickly, largely off-key, shouting at the top of her lungs, which, she explained, is the way she sings, just as that is the way (she also explained) countless other Americans sing.

No disrespect there, just an unexpected rendition in much the same way Jimi Hendrix's acoustic guitar rendition of "The Star Spangled Banner" and José Feliciano's avant-garde offering of the same song were misunderstood and caused unwarranted flaps.

After the song, however, Barr, doing the shtick of a ballplayer, grabbed her crotch and spat on the ground, an idea she got from the players and their wives while joking around prior to her performance.

Thinking she was being disrespectful to the nation, the thirty thousand fans in attendance booed her off the field. More than twelve hundred phone calls of complaint flooded the San Diego Padres' switchboard. Robert Merrill, the opera star and longtime anthemer at Yankee Stadium, called Roseanne's act deplorable and "outlandish." President

George Bush, the former Yale first baseman whose son owns the Texas Rangers, commented, "It was disgraceful."

Barr's comment afterward: "I wish I had performed it in front of a more hip crowd."

Tag line: The Padres, mired in a deep slump, 15 games below .500, swept both ends of the doubleheader by scores of 2–1 and 10–4. Did Kate Smith, who sang a lucky rendition of "God Bless America," for hockey's successful Philadelphia Flyers, start this way?

Bill Hands

Bill Hands, a steady right-handed pitcher for the Chicago Cubs (11-year career, 111 wins, 110 losses, and 1,128 strikeouts in 1,950 innings), let word leak out that he could perform hypnotism on the mound and induce opposing batters to strike out.

Hearing this, Pittsburgh Pirates hitters—whom he would face the next game—decided that if they didn't look at Hands, they couldn't be hypnotized and wouldn't strike out.

One thing, though: By not looking at Hands, they also did not see his pitches. Not seeing pitches can be fatal to a hitter.

The result: Hands pitched a one-hitter. Pittsburgh took its chances with hypnotism next time out. This must rank as one of the oddest and best psych jobs in baseball history.

Ryne Duren and Earl Averill

Generally when a wild pitch is thrown and the manager is angry, he'll take out the pitcher. Taking out the catcher is like shooting the messenger for bringing bad news. But Bill Rigney, manager of the expansion 1961 Los Angeles

Angels, saw that things weren't going well against the Washington Senators at Griffith Stadium. When bespectacled relief fireballer Ryne Duren let fly with a fast one that bounced down and away from catcher Earl Averill, Jr., two runs were scored and a close game was getting away.

Rigney stormed out to the mound for a conference. The able receiver, Averill (a seven-year catcher and son of Hall-of-Fame outfielder Earl Averill), explained, "He didn't tell me he was going to throw a spitter."

Rigney, going against tradition, left in the squinting reliever (two saves and a 5.19 ERA). It may be the first time in history a catcher was removed for not catching a spitter.

Eli Grba and Mickey Mantle

Another expansion Angels story deals with another pitcher with glasses, Eli Grba. In 1961, Grba (11–13 with a 4.25 ERA), an ex-Yankee, was pitching against his former teammates for the first time and, as a dutiful Angel, was going over the hitters with manager Rigney, when the skipper got to Yankee slugger Mickey Mantle.

Looking for weaknesses and a way to pitch to the switch-hitter, Grba announced, "When Mantle bats right-handed, throw him high; when he bats left-handed, pitch him low."

The Angel pitching staff agreed and pitched Mantle as Grba had instructed. The result: Up lefty, Mantle homered over the right-field wall; up righty, Mantle homered over the left-field wall.

Rigney looked to Grba, who was on the bench by this time, and Grba simply said, "Or was it the other way around?"

Dave Bresnahan

On August 31, 1987, second-string Minor League catcher Dave Bresnahan became an odd baseball immortal. On this night, in a game between his Williamsport (AA, Eastern League) team against Reading, he substituted a peeled potato for a baseball and tricked a Reading runner into leaving the bag on an apparent pickoff attempt.

With two outs in the ninth, Bresnahan called time and told the umpire his glove was broken. He exchanged the glove for a new one, with the peeled potato inside. He transferred the spud to his bare hand and called for the next pitch.

The pitch was a ball, and Bresnahan intentionally fired the potato over the head of third baseman Oscar Mejia. The spud hurtled out into left field and Rick Lundblade, the runner at third, dug in for home.

Bresnahan stood at the plate with the real ball in his grasp and tagged Lundblade out. The umpire called the runner safe and charged Bresnahan with an error. He was ejected from the game and fined fifty dollars.

Soon Bresnahan, hitting only .149, was cut from the team, but Williamsport held a promotion offering a seat to anyone who had one dollar and a potato. Seizing that opportunity, Bresnahan paid his fine with fifty potatoes, dumped on his manager's desk.

While Bresnahan was soon out of baseball, Williamsport held a "night" in his honor and even retired his number, 59, and painted it on the outfield fence.

Perhaps never before has a .149 hitter been so honored.

[*Author's note:* Dave Bresnahan is the grand-nephew of Hall-of-Fame catcher Roger Bresnahan.]

Other odd-but-trues to enhance baseball lore:

Mel Hall calls his big, oversized, and possibly illegally large outfielder's glove "Lucille." Rumor has it that the real Lucille was a robust woman by whom a young Mel was introduced to the "finer points" of intimate relationships.

The fastest nine-inning game in Major League history was played on September 28, 1919, at the Polo Grounds, with the **New York Giants** beating the **Philadelphia Phillies,** 6–1, behind the five-hit pitching of **Jesse Barnes** (25–9 that season). The game was completed in 51 minutes.

The fastest nine-inning game in organized baseball history was a 32-minute blaze-through in the Southern Association (Minor Leagues) on September 19, 1910.The game was played as an experiment to see just how fast a game could be played. The final score saw **Mobile** beating the **Atlanta Crackers** 2–1. During the game, hitters often swung at the first pitch, there was one walk, and no strikeouts. Mobile outhit Atlanta 6 to 4.

According to historian Jim Skipper, **John "Dots" Miller,** a second baseman who played from 1909 to 1921 for the Pittsburgh Pirates and the St. Louis Cardinals (.263 average), playing with Honus Wagner as his shortstop, acquired his odd nickname because of a misunderstanding. When a writer approached Wagner and asked who the young second baseman was, Wagner, in his heavy German accent, said, "Dots [That's] Miller." The writer took him literally and the nickname stuck.

Hall-of-Fame Chicago White Sox shortstop **Luke Appling** was patrolling the infield at Comisky Park during a game in the 1930s when he heard his spikes hit metal. The game was delayed as a huge blue-and-white copper kettle was removed from the infield and the resulting big hole was filled in. The site had formerly been a city dump.

At Wrigley Field in Chicago in 1969, Pittsburgh Pirate outfielder **Roberto Clemente** chased a Cubbie hit into the vines on the outfield wall. Clemente reached into the vines, pulled out a white sphere, and fired home. The throw died after about 20 feet. Clemente had picked up and thrown, not the ball, but an empty white Coca-Cola cup.

At Crosley Field in Cincinnati, following the Mill Creek Flood of 1937, which covered the playing field with 21 feet of water, Cincy pitchers **Lee Grissom** and **Gene Schott** rowed a boat over the center-field fence.

At Tiger Stadium (then known as Briggs Stadium), Detroit, in the seventh game of the 1937 World Series, **Ducky Medwick,** the left-fielder for the visiting St. Louis Cardinals, was pelted with fruits and vegetables thrown by fans in the stands, causing Commissioner **Kenesaw Mountain Landis** to remove him from the game for his own safety.

At Fenway Park, Boston, on May 17, 1947, Red Sox versus Browns, a sea gull cruised over the field and dropped a three-pound smelt on the mound, leaving St. Louis Browns hurler **Ellis Kinder** dumbstruck.

At Griffith Stadium in Washington, D.C., during a Senators-Tigers night game, with the pitcher on the mound and into his windup and a 2–2 count on the hitter, **George Kell,** the lights went out. When the lights came back on, all the infielders and outfielders, the umpire, the batter, and the catcher were lying flat on the ground. Only the pitcher was standing, because only he knew that he had not pitched the ball.

At Sick's Stadium in Seattle, Washington, in the opening game for the **Seattle Pilots,** April 11, 1969, fans were able to get a free view of the game by looking through the gaping openings of the unfinished board fence. More than seven thousand seats were unfinished at game time, and seven hundred fans had to wait an hour while carpenters finished their work, before they could sit in their seats.

Odd Deaths

The following lists are not funny; nor are they meant to be. But they chronicle the untimely demises of players (both active and retired) who gave their all on the field and were gone before their last licks in the ninth inning of life.

These memorials are believed to be the first public, published records of those who died under odd circumstances, which make their inclusion a logical addition to this chapter.

In an effort to maintain a certain amount of respect for the deceased, no additional comments will be offered, and only the cause of death will be given.

Accidental Deaths

SOURCE: Bill Deane & Rich Topp (SABR).

DATE	PLAYER (DEBUT)	CAUSE OF DEATH
Sep 01 1872	Al Thake (1872)	drowned, fell out of boat
May 11 1887	John Ake (1884)	drowned while trying to row Mississippi River
Nov 10 1888	John Glenn (1871)	shot by policeman protecting him from lynch mob
Mar 29 1894	Jim Gallagher (1886)	fall
Aug 13 1895	Bill Colgan (1884)	killed coupling railroad cars
Aug 03 1898	Emory Nusz (1884)	fell and crushed under train
Apr 28 1900	Walter Plock (1891)	bridge accident
Jul 17 1900	John Traffley (1889)	brain injury after fall
Jul 24 1900	Fred Zahner (1894)	drowned
Sep 14 1900	Ed Knouff (1885)	broken back two years after fighting fire

DATE	PLAYER (DEBUT)	CAUSE OF DEATH
Mar 10 1901	Charlie Snyder (1890)	evicted from hotel and fractured skull on sidewalk
Nov 16 1901	Jim Duncan (1899)	drowned
Apr 05 1902	Dave Eggler (1871)	hit by train
Feb 06 1903	Hardie Henderson (1883)	hit by streetcar
Jul 02 1903	Ed Delahanty (1888)	drowned, went over Niagara Falls
May 07 1905	Al Mays (1885)	drowned
Jun 30 1905	Pete Dowling (1897)	hit by train
Apr 21 1907	Nat Hicks (1872)	asphyxiated by gas in hotel room
Apr 26 1909	Mike Dorgan (1877)	blood poisoning from old ballplaying injury to leg
Jul 14 1910	Jack Horner (1894)	slipped in bath and fractured skull
Jul 05 1911	Jerry O'Brien (1887)	drowned
Aug 31 1911	Will White (1877)	drowned
Nov 22 1911	Ed Cermak (1901)	hit in throat with baseball while umpire
Dec 06 1911	Ed Glenn (1898)	fell in pit at locomotive repair shop
Jan 31 1912	Rube Taylor (1903)	skull crushed under streetcar wheels
Oct 12 1912	Charlie Waitt (1877)	fell while washing window
Nov 27 1912	Fred Corey (1878)	asphyxiated by gas in hotel room
Dec 31 1912	Charlie Sprauge (1887)	head injury in fall
Feb 10 1913	Joe Stewart (1904)	fell out of window
Jul 05 1914	Willie Mills (1901)	railroad accident
Nov 10 1914	Heinie Reitz (1893)	hit by auto
Nov 09 1915	Otis Johnson (1911)	shot self while hunting
Jun 09 1916	John Dodge (1912)	hit by pitched ball
Nov 29 1916	Bob Unglaub (1904)	crushed while working in railroad repair shop
Dec 30 1916	Reddy Mack (1885)	fell and fractured skull
May 25 1917	Willie Sudhoff (1897)	head injury from fall
Feb 11 1918	Carl Druhot (1906)	shipyard accident

DATE	PLAYER (DEBUT)	CAUSE OF DEATH
May 24 1918	Ralph Sharman (1917)	drowned
Oct 05 1918	Eddie Grant (1905)	killed in combat
Oct 07 1918	Bun Troy (1912)	killed in combat
Nov 01 1918	Alex Burr (1914)	killed in combat
Jun 05 1919	John McCloskey (1906)	mine explosion
Aug 21 1919	Bob Clark (1886)	burned
Oct 14 1919	Harry Blake (1894)	burned
Aug 17 1920	Ray Chapman (1912)	hit by pitched ball
Dec 16 1920	Dick Bayless (1908)	mine explosion
Dec 22 1921	Socks Seybold (1899)	auto accident
May 31 1922	John Coleman (1883)	hit by auto
Aug 16 1923	Jim Scoggins (1913)	brain injury developed after being hit by ball
Dec 09 1923	Wild Bill Donovan (1898)	train wreck
Feb 16 1924	Tony Boeckel (1917)	auto accident
Jun 02 1924	Jim Hughes (1898)	fell from train trestle and fractured skull
Sep 05 1925	Emil Huhn (1915)	team bus accident
Sep 21 1925	Charlie Irwin (1893)	hit by bus
Oct 22 1925	Marv Goodwin (1916)	military airplane crash
Feb 27 1926	Otis Clymer (1905)	auto accident
Dec 01 1927	Germany Smith (1884)	hit by auto
Feb 23 1928	Jack Ridgway (1914)	auto accident
Mar 14 1928	Nat Hudson (1886)	crushed while coupling streetcars
Mar 24 1929	Danny Claire (1920)	burned
Mar 24 1929	Denny Williams (1921)	auto accident
Apr 05 1929	Tom Crooke (1909)	bus accident
Apr 30 1929	Dan Long (1888)	railroad accident
July 20 1929	Rupert Mills (1915)	drowned
Oct 22 1929	Walt Lerian (1928)	truck jumped curb and pinned him to storefront
Feb 03 1930	Gus Sanberg (1923)	burned
Mar 12 1930	Jack Powell (1913)	choked in restaurant
Aug 15 1930	Guy Tutwhiler (1911)	hit by railroad trestle
Dec 29 1930	Sandy Piez (1914)	drowned after car went over bridge

DATE	PLAYER (DEBUT)	CAUSE OF DEATH
May 17 1931	Charlie Ferguson (1901)	drowned
Jan 17 1932	Mark Stewart (1913)	hit by drunk driver
Apr 23 1932	Lon Knight (1875)	asphyxiation by gas
May 23 1932	Doug Neff (1914)	drowned in boat accident
Jul 18 1932	Howard Freigau (1922)	drowned
Jul 02 1933	Tommy Dowd (1891)	drowned
Aug 28 1933	Fred Wood (1884)	hit by auto
Jan 28 1934	John Kane (1907)	auto accident
Feb 12 1934	Rowdy Elliott (1910)	fell from window
Mar 09 1934	Dan Dugdale (1886)	hit by truck
Mar 16 1934	Adrian Lynch (1920)	drove auto into ditch
Aug 11 1934	Joe Ward (1906)	auto accident
May 28 1935	Charlie Sullivan (1928)	auto-train accident
Nov 09 1935	Rex DeVogt (1913)	auto accident
Aug 13 1936	Irv Hach (1897)	fell from truck
Sep 11 1936	Braggo Roth (1914)	auto-truck accident
Oct 22 1936	Fred Olmstead (1908)	auto accident
Jan 15 1937	Eddie Foster (1910)	hit by auto
Feb 04 1937	Harry Wolverton (1898)	hit by auto
May 22 1937	Hi Jasper (1914)	fell off truck
Aug 31 1937	Gene Connell (1931)	auto accident
Nov 26 1937	Andy Bednar (1930)	auto accident
Dec 12 1937	Rube Benton (1910)	auto accident
Jan 16 1938	Earl Clark (1927)	auto-streetcar accident
Jan 28 1938	Still Bill Hill (1896)	auto accident
Feb 03 1938	Mike Donovan (1904)	accidentally shot by fellow guard at work
Mar 25 1939	Tiny Chaplin (1928)	auto accident
Nov 09 1939	Pete Henning (1914)	auto accident
Jun 24 1940	Axel Lindstrom (1916)	fractured skull from fall
Oct 23 1940	Harry Krause (1908)	auto accident
Dec 22 1940	Patsy McGaffigan (1917)	drowned
Jul 14 1941	Rube Kisinger (1902)	freak train accident while on duty as watchman
Sep 08 1941	Joe Boehling (1912)	fell from porch
Dec 15 1941	George Gilpatrick (1898)	fractured skull from fall
Apr 26 1942	Al Montgomery (1941)	auto accident

DATE	PLAYER (DEBUT)	CAUSE OF DEATH
Jun 30 1942	Cad Coles (1914)	drowned
Jul 08 1942	Harry Spies (1895)	hit by auto
Nov 29 1942	Bob Bescher (1908)	auto-train accident
Nov 30 1942	Slim Love (1913)	hit by auto
Dec 01 1942	Frank Connaughton (1894)	hit by auto
Dec 03 1942	Chad Kimsey (1929)	drove truck into bridge
Apr 15 1944	Elmer Gedeon (1939)	killed in combat
Nov 01 1944	Ed Brandt (1928)	hit by auto
Jan 05 1945	Bill Hobbs (1913)	shot while hunting
Mar 06 1945	Harry O'Neill (1939)	killed in combat
Mar 03 1946	Hick Cady (1912)	burned
May 07 1946	Bill Fincher (1916)	accidentally shot
May 23 1946	Johnny Grabowski (1924)	burned
Jun 26 1946	Chris Hartje (1939)	burned in Spokane team bus accident
Sep 16 1946	Emil Bildilli (1937)	drove auto into tree
Oct 04 1946	John Woods (1924)	drove auto into truck
Jan 15 1947	Jimmy Sheckard (1897)	hit by auto
Apr 12 1947	Tom Sullivan (1884)	hit by auto
Jul 16 1947	Bill Keen (1911)	auto-train accident
Aug 14 1947	Woody Crowson (1945)	team bus-truck accident
Dec 26 1947	Phil Stremmel (1909)	carbon monoxide poisoning
May 19 1948	Frank Browning (1910)	burned
Jul 01 1948	Pete Knisely (1912)	fell from railroad trestle
Aug 09 1948	Chuck Bowen (1919)	fell out of window
Oct 28 1948	Roy Ellam (1909)	hit by falling weight
Feb 08 1949	John Carden (1946)	electrocuted at work
Feb 18 1949	Marty O'Toole (1908)	fell down stairs
Oct 19 1949	Bill Steele (1910)	hit by streetcar
Mar 16 1950	Nub Kleinke (1935)	drowned while fishing
Sep 21 1950	Duke Kenworthy (1912)	drowned while fishing
Dec 06 1950	Jing Johnson (1916)	auto accident
Jul 14 1951	Vance Page (1938)	fractured skull from fall
Aug 17 1951	John Cameron (1906)	burned
Oct 12 1951	Rube Vinson (1904)	fell from window
Apr 05 1952	Ray Jacobs (1928)	auto accident
May 03 1952	Burt Keeley (1908)	fractured hip

DATE	PLAYER (DEBUT)	CAUSE OF DEATH
Aug 08 1952	Bob Neighbors (1939)	missing in combat
Aug 30 1952	Arky Vaughan (1932)	drowned
May 07 1954	Les Channell (1910)	fell at home
Oct 22 1954	Earl Whitehill (1923)	auto accident
Dec 17 1955	Rube DeGoff (1905)	auto accident
Jul 30 1956	Tommy Sewell (1927)	drowned
Sep 20 1956	Tommy Gastall (1955)	drowned after plane crash
Nov 27 1956	Charlie Peete (1956)	airplane crash
Feb 20 1957	Dixie Leverett (1922)	fell from tree
Mar 22 1957	Charlie Babington (1915)	injured in fall
Aug 25 1957	Ivy Griffin (1919)	auto accident
Jan 23 1958	Walt Lonergan (1911)	fractured skull from fall
Jun 09 1958	John Phillips (1945)	accidental electrocution
Jul 08 1958	Bill McAfee (1930)	airplane crash
Aug 21 1958	George Quellich (1931)	auto accident
Sep 15 1958	Snuffy Stirnweiss (1943)	train wreck
Sep 27 1958	Joe Berry (1942)	auto accident
Nov 09 1958	Walt Meinert (1913)	fell down loading shaft
Nov 21 1958	Mel Ott (1926)	auto accident
Feb 27 1959	Howie Fitzgerald (1922)	auto accident
Jul 29 1959	Boileryard Clarke (1893)	hip fracture
Sep 09 1959	Terry Lyons (1929)	asphyxiated with gas administered by dentist
Nov 28 1959	Ed McFarland (1893)	accidental fall
Feb 11 1960	Fritz Clausen (1892)	injured in fall
Feb 24 1960	Uke Clanton (1922)	auto accident
Mar 17 1960	Bob Thorpe (1955)	electrocuted at work
Jun 09 1962	Bill Thompson (1892)	fractured hip in fall
Sep 27 1962	Johnny Scalzi (1931)	auto accident
Oct 11 1962	Bill Bell (1952)	auto accident
Oct 16 1962	Possum Whitted (1912)	fractured hip in fall
May 22 1963	Dave Shean (1906)	drove auto into fence
Aug 13 1963	Karl Drews (1946)	hit by auto while changing tire
Nov 21 1963	Ed Hock (1920)	drowned
Dec 20 1963	Dinny McNamara (1927)	hit by auto
Feb 12 1964	Ted Pawelek (1946)	auto-truck accident

DATE	PLAYER (DEBUT)	CAUSE OF DEATH
Feb 15 1964	Ken Hubbs (1961)	airplane crash
Mar 02 1964	Fred Vaughn (1944)	auto accident
Mar 03 1964	Lefty Scott (1945)	fractured skull
Apr 13 1964	Ed Pipgras (1932)	auto accident
Oct 09 1964	Al Wingo (1919)	auto-truck accident
Jan 09 1965	Jim Joe Edwards (1922)	auto accident
Jun 20 1965	Jay Dahl (1963)	auto accident
Dec 15 1965	Dick Newsome (1941)	auto accident
Mar 04 1966	Jack Niemes (1943)	auto accident
May 03 1966	John Grady (1938)	auto accident
May 07 1966	Bing Miller (1921)	auto accident
July 22 1966	Frank Delahanty (1905)	fall causing hip and wrist injuries
Nov 24 1966	Tom Gulley (1923)	drowned
Jul 21 1967	Jimmie Foxx (1925)	choked on piece of meat
Apr 14 1968	Al Benton (1934)	burned
Jun 30 1968	Ned Porter (1926)	explosion on board boat
Sep 12 1968	Don Rudolph (1957)	crushed by dump truck
Mar 16 1969	Nestor Chavez (1967)	airplane crash
Jun 30 1969	Milt Gray (1937)	auto-train accident
Sep 18 1969	Joe Grace (1938)	four-car auto accident
Oct 02 1969	Danny O'Connell (1950)	auto accident
Nov 14 1969	Curt Roberts (1954)	hit by auto while changing tire
Feb 13 1970	Paul Edmondson (1969)	auto accident
Oct 23 1970	Sherry Robertson (1940)	auto accident
Dec 05 1970	Joe Wyatt (1924)	shot while hunting
Dec 14 1970	Herman Hill (1969)	drowned
Sep 11 1971	Rube Melton (1941)	auto accident
Feb 09 1972	Chico Ruiz (1964)	auto accident
Dec 31 1972	Roberto Clemente (1955)	airplane crash
Jan 26 1973	Pat Hardgrove (1918)	auto accident
Mar 12 1973	Frankie Frisch (1919)	auto accident
Nov 24 1974	Johnny Weekly (1962)	auto accident
Sep 03 1975	Irv Medlinger (1949)	airplane crash
Oct 08 1976	John Bottarini (1937)	drowned while fishing
Oct 09 1976	Bob Moose (1967)	auto accident

DATE	PLAYER (DEBUT)	CAUSE OF DEATH
Jan 01 1977	Danny Frisella (1967)	dune buggy accident
Jan 06 1977	Mike Miley (1975)	auto accident
May 11 1977	John Chambers (1937)	drowned while fishing
Jun 11 1977	Dick Farrell (1956)	auto accident
Aug 19 1977	Bob Klinger (1938)	auto accident
Sep 11 1978	Bob Gazella (1923)	auto accident
Aug 02 1979	Thurman Munson (1969)	airplane crash
Jul 08 1980	Wenty Ford (1973)	auto accident
Apr 12 1981	Dick Hoover (1952)	auto accident
Sep 27 1981	Al Bool (1928)	tractor overturned
Jun 13 1982	Randy Bobb (1968)	auto accident
Mar 12 1983	Bob Hall (1949)	hit by auto
Oct 28 1983	Ray Sanders (1942)	auto accident
Aug 14 1984	Lynn McGlothen (1972)	overcome by smoke in fire
Dec 20 1984	Gonzalo Marquez (1972)	auto accident
Mar 25 1985	Joe Wood (1943)	carbon monoxide and soot inhalation in fire
Jan 12 1986	Eddie Solomon (1973)	auto accident
Oct 12 1986	Norm Cash (1958)	drowned
Dec 20 1986	Joe DeSa (1980)	auto accident
Apr 27 1987	John Burrows (1943)	burned
Jul 24 1987	Fred Newman (1962)	auto accident
Nov 16 1987	Jim Brewer (1960)	auto accident
May 18 1989	Specs Toporcer (1921)	fall
Dec 25 1989	Billy Martin (1950)	auto accident
Jul 07 1990	Don Bessent (1955)	alcohol poisoning
Nov 22 1990	Bo Diaz	crushed by satellite dish

Murders

SOURCE: Bill Deane & Rich Topp (SABR).

DATE	PLAYER (DEBUT)	CAUSE OF DEATH
Apr 18 1885	Ted Firth (1884)	method unknown
Apr 14 1891	Frank Bell (1885)	gunshot
Jan 25 1895	Frank Bowes (1890)	gunshot
Feb 15 1897	Fleury Sullivan (1884)	shot during political row

DATE	PLAYER (DEBUT)	CAUSE OF DEATH
Nov 23 1898	Mother Watson (1887)	gunshot
June 12 1900	Mox McQuery (1884)	shot by thug
Mar 22 1902	John Ryan (1873)	kicked to death while making arrest
Mar 12 1907	Pat Hynes (1903)	shot by bartender over credit on two beers
Apr 23 1911	George Craig (1907)	shot by burglar
Sep 07 1912	Bugs Raymond (1904)	hit with baseball bat in tavern brawl
Apr 16 1913	Jerry Harrington (1890)	method unknown
Feb 18 1916	Ed Irvin (1912)	thrown out of saloon to die on street
Mar 14 1921	Larry McLean (1901)	shot by bartender
Jun 11 1922	Chief Johnson (1913)	gunshot
Sep 01 1923	Frank McManus (1899)	method unknown
Dec 01 1924	Dolly Stark (1909)	shot in saloon brawl
Jan 27 1927	Drummond Brown (1913)	gunshot
Mar 03 1932	Ed Morris (1922)	stabbed during party in his honor
Sep 17 1935	Len Koenecke (1932)	battered with fire extinguisher by plane pilot in self-defense
Oct 12 1935	Ray Treadway (1930)	gunshot
Aug 06 1942	Gordon McNaughton (1932)	shot by jealous husband in hotel room
Jul 02 1945	Frank Grube (1931)	shot by prowler
Jan 01 1952	Hi Bithorn (1942)	shot by policeman
Oct 09 1955	Howie Fox (1944)	stabbed in tavern brawl
Jun 18 1961	Eddie Gaedel (1951)	heart attack after being beaten by thugs
Aug 20 1969	Tim McKeithan (1932)	gunshot
Jan 29 1970	Mickey Fuentes (1969)	shot in tavern brawl
Apr 11 1974	Bob Baird (1962)	shot during quarrel with woman
Sep 24 1978	Lyman Bostock (1975)	gunshot
Mar 29 1979	Luke Easter (1949)	shot during robbery
Mar 31 1979	Bob Schultz (1951)	shot in tavern
Nov 22 1983	Dave Short (1940)	beaten, found in car trunk
Feb 01 1988	Luis Marquez (1951)	shot during family quarrel
Feb 10 1990	Tony Solaita (1968)	shot over land dispute

Suicides

SOURCE: Bill Deane & Rich Topp (SABR).

DATE	PLAYER (DEBUT)	CAUSE OF DEATH
May 10 1881	Fraly Rogers (1872)	gunshot
Feb 24 1889	Jim McElroy (1884)	opium overdose
Apr 12 1889	Frank Ringo (1883)	morphine overdose
Nov 22 1891	Ernie Hickman (1884)	gunshot
Feb 28 1894	Edgar McNabb (1893)	gunshot after killing his mistress
Sep 16 1894	Terry Larkin (1876)	razor
Sep 19 1896	Cannonball Crane (1884)	drank chloral
Jan 19 1900	Marty Bergen (1896)	razor after killing wife and children with ax
Apr 30 1901	Dude Esterbrook (1880)	jumped from train en route to mental hospital
Jan 12 1903	Win Mercer (1894)	gas
Feb 01 1904	Dan Mahoney (1892)	drank carbolic acid
Jan 10 1907	Bob Langsford (1899)	drank carbolic acid
Mar 28 1907	Chick Stahl (1897)	drank carbolic acid
Sep 14 1908	Ike Van Zandt (1901)	gunshot
Dec 19 1908	Reddy Foster (1896)	gunshot
Dec 13 1910	Dan McGann (1895)	gunshot
Jan 18 1911	Dick Scott (1901)	razor
Jan 11 1914	Walt Goldsby (1884)	gunshot
Jun 13 1914	Charlie Weber (1898)	gunshot
Mar 28 1916	Eddie Hohnhurst (1910)	method unknown
May 15 1918	Patsy Tebeau (1887)	gunshot
Nov 30 1920	Lew Meyers (1884)	strychnine
Jul 16 1921	Art Irwin (1880)	jumped ship in ocean
Mar 16 1927	Jake Wells (1888)	method unknown
Apr 26 1927	Bill Gannon (1898)	drowning
Dec 01 1927	Danny Shay (1901)	method unknown
Aug 05 1929	Tony Brottem (1916)	gunshot
Jul 16 1930	Zeke Rosebraugh (1898)	gunshot
Jun 25 1931	Con Lucid (1893)	method unknown
Sep 11 1931	Carl Sitton (1909)	gunshot

DATE	PLAYER (DEBUT)	CAUSE OF DEATH
Dec 08 1932	Bill Grey (1890)	gunshot
Mar 21 1934	Pea Ridge Day (1924)	gunshot
Jun 09 1934	Charlie Dexter (1896)	gunshot
Aug 14 1934	Guy Morrison (1927)	gunshot
Jun 14 1935	Walt Kuhn (1912)	gunshot
Apr 15 1937	Emmett McCann (1920)	gunshot
Nov 01 1937	Benny Frey (1929)	carbon monoxide
Aug 03 1940	Will Hershberger (1938)	razor
Aug 14 1940	Charlie Hollocher (1918)	gunshot
Aug 08 1941	Ralph Works (1909)	gunshot after killing wife
Oct 29 1941	Harvey Hendrick (1923)	method unknown
Aug 05 1942	Lyle Bigbee (1920)	gunshot
Jun 23 1943	Chet Chadbourne (1906)	gunshot
Nov 11 1945	Harry McNeal (1901)	gunshot
Oct 16 1945	Hank Eibel (1912)	gunshot
Nov 18 1945	Morrie Rath (1909)	gunshot
Jun 15 1947	Luke Stuart (1921)	gunshot
Jul 18 1948	Bert Hall (1911)	hanging
Nov 04 1948	Jake Powell (1930)	gunshot
Oct 25 1949	Tim Bowden (1914)	gunshot
May 19 1950	Wattie Holm (1924)	gunshot
Sept 03 1950	Frank Pearce (1950)	gunshot
Jul 03 1951	Hugh Casey (1935)	gunshot
Sep 14 1951	Wally Roettger (1927)	razor
Jan 09 1954	Skeeter Shelton (1915)	gunshot
Sep 01 1955	Jim Oglesby (1946)	gunshot
Nov 01 1956	Limb McKenry (1915)	gunshot
Nov 08 1957	Fred Anderson (1909)	gunshot
Jan 20 1960	Gib Brack (1937)	gunshot
Jun 04 1961	George Davis (1912)	hanging
Nov 24 1961	John Mohardt (1922)	cut femoral artery
Jan 10 1962	Fred Bratchi (1921)	drank battery acid
Mar 29 1962	Otto Miller (1910)	jumped
Jun 28 1962	Cy Morgan (1903)	razor
Sep 16 1963	Johnny Niggeling (1938)	hanging
Sep 26 1964	Paul Zahniser (1923)	gunshot
Aug 15 1965	Stan Pitula (1957)	carbon monoxide

DATE	PLAYER (DEBUT)	CAUSE OF DEATH
Nov 02 1966	Lew Moren (1903)	cut throat
Oct 19 1967	Art Garibaldi (1936)	gunshot
Nov. 25 1969	Emil Kush (1941)	carbon monoxide
Oct 08 1971	Murray Wall (1950)	gunshot
Jun 09 1972	Del Bissonette (1928)	gunshot
Jan 05 1975	Don Wilson (1966)	carbon monoxide
Jun 12 1980	Danny Thomas (1976)	hanging
Apr 09 1982	Francisco Barrios (1974)	heroin overdose
Apr 06 1989	Carlos Bernier (1953)	hanging
Jul 18 1989	Donnie Moore (1975)	gunshot

Bibliography

Some of the information contained in this book was reinforced by the various accounts of similar oddities and rituals published in the following books, magazines, articles, and newspapers:

Fuselle, Warner. *Baseball: A Laughing Matter.* St. Louis, MO: The Sporting News, 1987.

Gutman, Dan. *It Ain't Cheatin' If You Don't Get Caught.* New York: Penguin Books, 1990.

Hershberger, Chuck. *Old Tyme Baseball News.* Pleasant Ridge, MI: Where Sports Network. Numerous articles from several editions 1987–1990.

The Los Angeles Times, Los Angeles, CA. Many clips from numerous editions 1989–1990.

Lowry, Philip J. *Green Cathedrals.* Manhattan KS: SABR, Ag Press, 1986.

Major League Baseball, *The Major League Baseball Newsletter.* Commissioner's Office, New York. Editions of April, May, June, July, 1990.

Mote, James. *Everything Baseball.* New York: Prentice Hall Press, 1989.

Nash, Bruce, and Allan Zullo. *The Baseball Hall of Shame.* New York: Pocket Books, 1985.

Nash, Bruce, and Allan Zullo. *The Baseball Hall of Shame.* New York: Pocket Books, 1986.

Nash, Bruce, and Allan Zullo. *The Baseball Hall of Shame.* New York: Pocket Books, 1987.

Nash, Bruce, and Allan Zullo. *The Baseball Hall of Shame.* New York: Pocket Books 1990.

Obojski, Robert. *Baseball's Strangest Moments.* New York: Sterling Publishing Co., 1988.

Obojski, Robert. *Bush League: A History of Minor League Baseball.* New York: Macmillan Publishing Co., 1975.

Okrent, Daniel, and Steve Wulf. *Baseball Anecdotes.* New York: Harper & Row (reprinted by permission of Oxford University Press), 1989.

The Orange County Register. Santa Ana, CA. Many clips from numerous editions, 1989–1990.

Peary, Danny. *Cult Baseball Players.* New York: Simon and Schuster, 1990.

Reichler, Joseph L., editor. *The Baseball Encyclopedia,* 7th ed. New York: Macmillan Publishing Co., 1988.

SABR (Society for American Baseball Research). *The SABR Bulletin* (Newsletter), vol. 20, no. 1; vol. 20, nos. 2 and 3. Garrett Park, MD, 1990.

Shlain, Bruce. *Oddballs.* New York: Penguin Books, 1989.

Shlossberg, Dan. *The Baseball Catalog.* Middle Village, NY: Jonathan David Publishers, Inc., 1980.

Shyer, Brent. *Dodgers Alumni News* 6, no. 2. Los Angeles, CA: Los Angeles Dodgers, 1990.

The Sporting News. St. Louis, MO. Many clips from numerous editions, 1987–1990.

Wolff, Rich, editorial director. *The Baseball Encyclopedia,* 8th ed. New York: Macmillan Publishing Co., 1990.

And the media guides and team magazines supplied by the following organizations:

Major League Baseball:
The 1990 Major League Baseball Media Information Guide. Commissioner's Office, New York, 1990.

American League:
American League Red Book, Baltimore Orioles, Boston Red Sox, California Angels, Chicago White Sox, Cleveland Indians, Detroit Tigers, Milwaukee Brewers, Minnesota Twins, New York Yankees, Oakland A's, Seattle Mariners, Texas Rangers, Toronto Blue Jays.

National League:
National League Green Book, Atlanta Braves, Chicago Cubs, Cincinnati Reds, Houston Astros, Los Angeles Dodgers, Montreal Expos, New York Mets, Philadelphia Phillies, Pittsburgh Pirates, St. Louis Cardinals, San Diego Padres, San Francisco Giants.

Index of Nam

Labine, Clem, 93
Laga, Mike, 147
Lajoie, Napoleon, 136
Lamp, Dennis, 151
Landis, Kenesaw Mountain, 177
Landreaux, Ken, 154
Landrum, Tito, 154
Langsford, Bob, 188
Lanier, Max, 66–67
Lardner, Ring, 109
Larkin, Terry, 188
Lasorda, Tommy, 72
Lee, Bill "Spaceman", 120–21
Leonard, Jeffrey, 89
Lerian, Walt, 181
Lesley, Brad "The Animal," 120
Leverett, Dixie, 184
Lind, Jose, 51, 129
Lindstrom, Axel, 182
Linz, Phil, 154–55
Lockman, Whitey, 60, 152
Loes, Billy, 45
Logan, Johnny, 65
Lollar, Sherman, 73
Lonergan, Walt, 184
Long, Dan, 181
Lopat, Ed, 60
Lotshaw, Andy, 155
Love, Slim, 183
Lucid, Con, 188
Lundblade, Rick, 176
Lyle, Sparky, 133, 157, 162
Lyons, Steve, 161
Lyons, Ted, 85
Lyons, Terry, 184
Lynch, Adrian, 182
Lynn, Fred, 153

MacDonald, Ben, 120
Mack, Connie, 57–58, 159
Mack, Reddy, 180
Maglie, Sal "The Barber," 47, 60
Mahoney, Dan, 188
Maldonado, Candy, 77
Mantle, Mickey, 30, 60, 90, 143–44, 154, 175
Maranville, "Rabbit," 33–34
Marberry, Firpo, 106
Marion, Marty, 71–72
Maris, Roger, 90, 144
Marquez, Gonzalo, 186
Marquez, Luis, 187
Marsans, Armando, 81
Martin, Billy, 145, 186
Martin, "Pepper," 25–26
Mattingly, Don, 74, 155
Mauch, Gene, 32, 34–35, 44, 58–59
May, Carlos, 52
Mays, Al, 180
Mays, Willie, 40, 60
McAfee, Bill, 184
McCann, Emmett, 189
McCarthy, Joe, 164–65
McCloskey, John, 181
McDonald, Tex, 81
McDowell, Roger, 51, 101, 118
McDougald, Gil, 60
McElroy, Jim, 188
McFarland, Ed, 184
McGaffigan, Patsy, 182
McGann, Dan, 188
McGlothen, Lynn, 186
McGowan, Bill, 37, 106
McGraw, Frank Edwin "Tug," 105

About the Author

Mike Blake is a sportswriter-screenwriter who has written for such literary giants as the *LA Herald Examiner, Classic Sports, Oui,* and Japan's *Mainichi* and *Sankei.*

His own Major League baseball career was cut short following some rather unique approaches to batting and fielding in high school and college—during which time he set a team record for walks—by what he terms "nothing more than a lack of talent."

Blake discovered the zany world of baseball superstitions, rituals, and oddities while interviewing countless ballplayers over the years. He even tried a few himself: The switch-hitting shortstop would "clang" his wrist sweat bands together for strength—"It worked for Wonder Woman," he says—and he still wears '60s-style Hawaiian puka shells around his neck, "as a nostalgic link to my youth, and a fervent hope to return to the Islands."

Blake grew up as a baseball switch-hitter—"Everyone in my New Jersey neighborhood of the late '50s was a switch-hitter," he says, "as homage to Mickey Mantle, and local teenage hero Butch Bellon"—but he writes right-handed—"I'm a switch-typist," he concedes. He can, however, look at the world left-handed, as you may discover as the author of more than five-hundred published articles, several books, and a dozen screenplays and TV treatments leaves the serious world behind and plunges, instead, into the funny world of baseball superstitions, rituals, and oddities.

Says the author, "If we can combine baseball with a few laughs, we've created the perfect world . . . or at least an entertaining book."